Evil Religions Unmasked

Oppression Torture Genocide

Through the Millennia

Eloy Rodrigo Colombo

2020

ISBN

      978-1-7349190-0-4 (paperback)
      978-1-7349190-4-2 (e-book EPUB)
      978-1-7349190-5-9 (e-book Mobipocket)
      978-1-7349190-6-6 (PDF)

Library of Congress Control TXu002185443 / 2020-02-15

Permission to use material from other works

1st Edition, 2020.

*To share discoveries with all people is more important
than maybe people think.
Like that, tell everyone who you like about this book!
Every word matters.*

Email: eloy@wecolombo.com

Join us at **wecolombo.com** and our group on Facebook
(you can search for the author's name or the book's name)

Twitter: @eloy_colombo

Contents

Preface

Our society teaches us numerous taboos, including the many issues that people do not like or do not know how to talk about without feeling embarrassed. To avoid these uncomfortable feelings, we generally avoid talking about taboos.

There are probably no stricter taboos than those on the subject of religion. Let me refresh your mind with some alarming questions that most people shy away from.

Why do so many people around the world claim that the Bible teaches that there is only one God in the universe when the Bible actually includes many passages like Exodus 20: "*You shall have **no other Gods** but me*"?

In fact, the Bible is full of phrases attesting the existence of many gods, phrases like Deuteronomy 13:

> *"If your brother, the son of your mother, or your son or your daughter or the wife you embrace or your friend who is as your own soul entices you secretly, saying, 'Let us go and serve **other gods**,' which neither you nor your fathers have known, some of the **gods** of the peoples who are around you, whether near you or far off from you, from the one end of the earth to the other, you shall not yield to him or listen to him, nor shall your eye pity him, nor shall you spare him, nor shall you conceal him. But you shall **kill** him."*

If we are to base our beliefs solely on the Bible, then no one can dare to affirm that there is only one God in the universe.

Another taboo question is why so many of us believe that the spiritual beings who have appeared to the prophets were good beings simply because these apparitions have called themselves God, angels, or the envoys of a god? In other words, why is it accepted as a sure fact that these apparitions are good spirits although we know nothing about them other than the powers they have displayed?

When a spirit identifying itself as God commands a prophet to kill people in God's name, as in the passage from Deuteronomy above, why should any person who hears this respond with automatic obedience? We should instead respond with prudent suspicion:

"If you are a powerful god and you are urging me to destroy some of the divine creation, I have only one thing to tell you: I myself am not great or powerful enough to judge whether you are really the creator of all things, or if you are even one of many gods with the power to create, nor can I judge whether the power to manifest yourself like this is proof that you are a god at all. Therefore, if you are really the all-powerful creator of all things and you desire to destroy something that you have created or if you are some being authorized by the creator-god to destroy His creation, you must go with your own awesome power and use it to destroy, kill, torture, and commit genocide by yourself. I will not do that on your behalf."

In fact, can we safely esteem the prophets as "wise" if they were not modest or prudent enough to question their own visions and ask these questions themselves?

However, the taboo aspects of religious belief go further.

How can people overlook the fact that more *human sacrifice* has been committed by the devotees of the three Abrahamic religions—Judaism, Christianity, and Islam—than by any other group in history? Even the Bible reports the many terrible genocides that have been committed in the name of Abraham's God!

Did all of the so-called prophets actually experience the spiritual apparitions they reported? Is it not possible that some of them were lying when they told people they had seen a god or a god's envoy? In many cases, the prophets were alone when they saw these apparitions.

These questions demand answers.

Furthermore, it has been discovered that many of the Abrahamic texts that the prophets claimed were the word of God were in reality copied from ancient Egyptian wisdom literature, including the Ten Commandments.

Were it not for the discovery of the Rosetta Stone and the deciphering of hieroglyphs in 1822, we would never have known that many of the Jewish, Christian, and Muslim holy texts were drawn from the ancient Egyptian wisdom literature that had come before them.

As you can see, we have a lot of religious taboos to break if we are to uncover the true history behind the globally dominant Abrahamic religions. This book will lead us through the difficult questions and attempt to answer a crucial question: is Abrahamic monotheism the biggest fraud in human history?

Introduction

It is widely accepted that the discord that has created the ongoing wars and conflicts in our world is an inherent part of human society. For thousands of years, humanity has found it difficult to live together in harmony. Our human environment has been characterized by the following:

- Intolerance
- Hatred
- Genocide

Many intellectuals have written about the causes of this behavior, but none have ever found the root of our problems. René Guenon, an influential scholar of comparative religion, claims that our modern world is typically interpreted only in terms of numbers, including financial data, and that there is a widespread disregard for the inherent quality of things. I maintain that this is not the cause of our problems but rather the direct consequence of a larger issue.

Another scholar who addressed this subject was Bertrand de Juvenel, a French philosopher and political economist. In his book *On Power: The Natural History of Its Growth*, de Juvenel explained the astonishing influence of governments and how their political authority has grown over the centuries. Although he understood the pattern of human conflict, he likewise never found the root cause.

This raises the question: What was, and is, the problem that prevents most modern intellectuals from finding the root cause of our intolerance, hatred, and genocidal tendencies?

In general, most Western intellectuals have never questioned Abrahamic monotheism because from their cultural perspective, monotheism is the superior religion. Even scholars who are themselves atheists tend to assume that if belief in one god is a sign of weakened intelligence, believing in many of them must be even worse.

From this book's shocking argument, you will see that modern Western intellectuals, including atheists, always begin their research from a monotheistic perspective founded on Abrahamic principles. Unfortunately, even those intellectuals who respect monotheistic religion nevertheless consider polytheistic religions such as the ancient Egyptian religion to be outdated and inferior, or even primitive and funny.

This is a big mistake!

Once you begin to question Abrahamic monotheism, however, you can clearly see where the root of our modern problems is located.

Analyses questioning the role of monotheism in leading us to conflagration are really few and scattered: I have found only one book centered on this issue published in the recent decades, offered by the author Jonathan Kirsch, who, as expected, identifies monotheism as the major overlooked cause of modern conflicts in his book *God against the Gods: The History of the War Between Monotheism and Polytheism*. Several other scholars appear to think that they understand how monotheism has contributed to our modern problems, but this author is one of only a very few to actually analyze the question. Although Kirsch gives a very interesting historical analysis, I have taken it further to write an ontological, phenomenological, cosmological, and literary analysis that examines the world from the perspective of the ancient Egyptian polytheistic cosmology, which was the dominant mindset in North Africa and western Asia when the Abrahamic religion emerged.

In this thesis, I will explore the possibility that the cause of the problems in our modern world is the monotheistic Abrahamic tradition and the religions that have developed from it, namely, Judaism, Christianity, and Islam.

Tragically, as we will see, the Abrahamic scriptures teach intolerance, hatred, and genocide. Likewise, every materialistic theory was an inevitable outcome of the Abrahamic tradition and religions. The materialistic theories are the inevitable daughters of those belief systems.

Another premise I will defend here is that polytheism is inevitable. This is because, even now, no one is worshiping or serving only one being or principle. Without realizing it, most people, even self-proclaimed monotheists and atheists, are worshiping many ideals and values as if they were gods. If you find it hard to understand how the ancient Egyptians could follow many gods, consider that today, most people are worshiping the political state, technology, science, brands, sports teams, music groups, and many other things, showering them with attention, money, and loyalty as if they were gods.

If you do not see this yet, I can provide many examples. Has anyone ever told you that *you need to comply with the law* regardless of whether the law is fair or just? Most people believe it is right to comply with the law even when the laws are immoral. For example, take the controversial laws against immigration: are immigrants being immoral when they try to better their lives in another country? Or consider the harsh laws against prostitution: is it ethical to jail someone for selling their own sexual services when this choice affects them alone? Are they really committing a crime in the sense of harming others? This attitude is a prime example of how people regard the law as sacred in and of itself, regardless of its contents, just as they would even worship a god who commanded terrible acts against their fellow humans. Doesn't this excessive regard for the law resemble the notion that *you need to comply with the sacred commandments of the Holy Scriptures because if you do not you, will be punished by God?*

And what about politicians? Don't they resemble priests in terms of the authority that they hold? People try to choose the perfect candidate to vote for as if making the right choice on the ballot will solve all of their problems. Isn't the state like a modern religion in this way, with its official buildings in the role of modern temples? Isn't the national anthem a prayer to the divine state?

Furthermore, many people's devotion to their favorite sports teams looks a great deal like a religion. Sports fans dedicate a great deal of time and money to following their teams and proving their loyalty.

If you think that the ancient Egyptian religion and way of thinking were not intelligent, keep reading and you will understand how rational they were, and how the devotees of these ancient ways would never fall into many of our modern traps.

The most intelligent aspect of the ancient Egyptian philosophy is its teaching that everything in our world is a manifestation of a divine power. They realized that the state, technology, medicines, social phenomena, natural phenomena, and everything else that exists in our world are all expressions of divine powers. They never looked at anything in the world as completely profane as we commonly do in modern times.

The goal of Egyptian polytheistic religion was to reach and maintain equilibrium in both nature and society. They believed it was the responsibility of all human beings to work toward that goal.

Here, I will guide you through a wonderful journey into the ancient world where religion was not merely one aspect of life but was understood to contain and suffuse all things, where religious faith and practice were never seen as matters of personal choice because everything was a manifestation of some god's power on earth.

Only this perspective can give you the ability to understand how the Abrahamic religions have twisted human's lives and to see their role in leading us over millennia to build a world of intolerance, hatred, and genocide.

A Brief History of the Egyptian and Roman Civilizations and their Similar Fates due to an Abrahamic Religion

When and where did our modern society begin to take the shape it has today?

A good place to look when attempting to answer this question is at the collapse of the Roman and ancient Egyptian civilizations.

Today, we struggle to make our governments endure for mere four years at a time; how then did the Roman civilization last more than 1,100 years? How did the ancient Egyptian civilization endure for more than 3,000 years?

Certainly, these societies endured many periods of crisis, some perhaps more severe than what we face today, but they overcame every one until each civilization faced its final pivotal crisis that overwhelmed them to such a degree that their civilizations were annihilated. Not only their governments but also each civilization's entire tradition, culture, religion, and habits were vanished from the Earth.

It strikes me as odd that intellectuals always try to find the causes of the collapses of these two great civilizations in political events such as the actions of powerful families, external influences such as barbarian incursions, or even social issues such as economic collapse. Explanations like these are sufficient to explain the collapse of an individual regime or the fall of a great family from power, but we are talking about the failure of two great and powerful civilizations that had lasted for millennia. The true explanation must center on something with enough power to penetrate so deeply as to destroy a whole civilization in its complexity.

Intellectuals rarely question the role of religion in the annihilation of these civilizations because, in our modern world, religion is separated from every other sphere of our lives. However this was never the case in ancient times.

The life of ancient peoples was immersed in religion to such a degree that a Roman or an ancient Egyptian would never understand how we can discuss religion as distinct from the rest of our lives. They would never understand how we think of religion as something we can choose to add to our lives like a hobby or reject it.

Below I present brief histories of the Roman and ancient Egyptian civilizations as we begin our extensive journey into the ancient world that will enable us to understand the role of Abrahamic monotheism in our modern problems.

Roman Civilization

753 BCE	Roman civilization began to emerge.
509 BCE	The Roman Republic was founded, ruled by senators. A constitution was established.
45 BCE	Julius Caesar won the civil war and established himself as imperator for life. He was assassinated the following year.
27 BCE	The Roman Empire emerged, ending the approximate 500-year tradition of the Republic.
306 CE	Constantine became both a Christian and the emperor. In 313 CE Constantine issued the Edit of Milan, ending the persecution of Christians.
380 AD	Theodosius issued the Edict of Thessalonica, making Christianity the official religion of the Roman Empire. Thereafter, the practice of polytheism was gradually forbidden in Roman territory, temples were closed, and polytheists were persecuted.
395 AD	The Roman Empire was divided into the Western Roman Empire and the Eastern Roman Empire.
476 AD	The Western Roman Empire ended, and the Middle Ages began.

In summary, the Roman civilization thrived under polytheism for more than 1000 years, from 753 BCE to 380 CE. This polytheistic way of life yielded astonishing cultural development, wealth production, and knowledge accumulation. Less than 100 years after the practice of monotheism was imposed, however, the Roman civilization had ended.

It is important to note that the Romans not only had their own polytheistic religion but also embraced and welcomed the religions of other cultures, often incorporating something of them into their own practices. The only one religion that was seen as a threat to their own was Christianity. I will analyze this in depth later on.

Egyptian Civilization

It is estimated that the ancient Egyptian civilization began to take shape around 5,000 BCE and ended around 600 CE, less than 300 years after the Christianized Roman Empire imposed Christianity on Egypt in its attempt to erase polytheistic culture from its jurisdiction.

Astonishingly, the Egyptian civilization thus lasted for around 5,600 years! The ancient Egyptian culture was so powerful that even invaders like the Persians, Greeks, and Romans respected it and tried to absorb some of its culture and traditions.

One thing to keep in mind about ancient times is that in general, conquerors did not forcefully interfere in local religion, tradition, cultural habits, or any other sphere outside politics. This seems to be a paradox given that ancient peoples believed that everything fell within the realm of religion. One might expect that conquerors would have pushed for their own religions and traditions to those of the seized lands. But this was not the case: rather than attempting to change local religion, the new rulers instead aimed to depict themselves as blending into local society. In Egypt, for example, there are many depictions of Roman emperors in the traditional garb of the Pharaohs. Thus, the conquerors wanted to defeat their opponents just in political terms only and did not try to change the local culture.

Egypt was first conquered by outsiders in 525 BCE when the Persians invaded. Later, the Persians were defeated by Alexander the Great, who captured Egypt in 332 BCE. After his death, his general Ptolemy made himself the king of Egypt. The Ptolemy family ruled Egypt for almost 300 years.

The last Ptolemaic ruler in Egypt was Cleopatra. When the Romans conquered Egypt in 30 BCE, some elements of Egyptian culture, including their gods, were absorbed by the Romans.

In ancient times, the Egyptian city of Alexandria was the cultural and scientific center of the Western world. This city, which had been founded by Alexander the Great following his annexation of Egypt, was the intellectual heart of the Western world for many centuries. The cultural dominance of Alexandria means that all knowledge of the ancient West converged there, rather than Alexandria spreading the knowledge of the ancient Egyptians to the rest of the world.

In 42 CE, Christianity began to spread into Egypt through the teachings of Mark the Evangelist. This strictly monotheistic faith was in opposition to the freely syncretic religious practice common in Egyptian culture. When Christianity spread and became the state religion of the Roman Empire, other religions, and gods were prohibited. The persecution of religions other than Christianity began in 381 CE. The authorities responsible for dismantling Egyptian polytheism were the bishops, monks, and priests who were also the leaders of Christianity.

The mortal blow happened in 642 CE, when Egypt was invaded and conquered by the Arab Islamic Empire sealing the end of the Egyptian polytheism; after that, the Egypt's power disappeared.

The eradication of ancient Egyptian polytheism was achieved through many means. The State support for traditional religion was ended, temple estates and properties were seized by those religious enemies, the polytheist priests and devotees were prohibited from practicing their religion publicly or privately, and the temples themselves were either converted to Christian or Islam temples or destroyed so that their stones could be used to build Abrahamic ones.

Why can only a religion explain the fall of the Roman and ancient Egyptian civilizations?

Can you imagine how many crises these two civilizations must have endured to survive as long as they did? Pests, riots, wars, agricultural setbacks such as droughts, floods, and plagues, political problems such as bad governors, public budget imbalances, political changes, economic issues, etc. They overcame all these problems for more than one thousand years in one case and more than three thousand years in the other.

But at that time wherein every sphere of life was immersed in religion, an issue that had formerly been no problem became a major obstacle.

In a polytheistic tradition, every god has a place in the pantheon, and the pantheon always has space for one more. This is not the case for the new religions that insist on only one god, such as Judaism, Christianity, or Islam.

As we will see in this book, analyzing the Abrahamic sacred texts in greater detail, the Abrahamic God does not admit any other god as His companion. Below are passages from Bible demonstrating this.

In Exodus 20, we read these words from the prophet Moses: *"You shall have **no other gods** but me."*

In Deuteronomy 13, the Abrahamic God commands the violent death of anyone who encourages Israelites to worship other gods.

> *"If your brother, the son of your mother, or your son or your daughter or the wife you embrace or your friend who is as your own soul entices you secretly, saying, 'Let us go and serve **other gods**,' which neither you nor your fathers have known, some of the **gods** of the peoples who are around you, whether near you or far off from you, from the one end of the earth to the other, you shall not yield to him or listen to him, nor shall your eye pity him, nor shall you spare him, nor shall you conceal him. But **you shall kill him**."*

In John 14, Jesus, whom Christians worship as God incarnate, said:

> *"**I am** the **way**, and the **truth**, and the **life**. No one comes to the Father **except through me**. If you had known me, you would have known my Father also. From now on, you do know Him and have **seen** Him."*

As if it was not enough, in Matthew 28, Jesus said:

> *"**All authority** in **heaven** and on **earth** has been given to me. Therefore, go and make disciples of all nations, baptizing them in the name of the Father and of the Son and of the Holy Spirit, and teaching them to **obey everything** I have commanded you. And surely I am with you always, to the very end of the age."*

Consequently, once Christianity had conquered the hearts of the Roman emperors, they were bound to do their utmost to crush every religion other than Christianity for two reasons: first, this was commanded by their God; second, at that time everything was inside the religious domain.

In the era of polytheistic predominance, the effects of political changes and conquests were often limited to the elite and military circles. The basic structure of society, in contrast, was hardly affected. In the era of Abrahamic monotheistic predominance, however, this was not possible as monotheistic rulers aimed to interfere forcefully in the foundation and structure of each society they ruled, imposing their own beliefs with no room for tolerance or freedom of thought and customs.

Later, we will see that this was why the modern separation of religion from practically every other area of life was an unavoidable outcome of living under Abrahamic monotheism for centuries. Polytheism enables tolerance and acceptance and can lead to harmony in society, whereas monotheism nourishes intolerance, hatred, and persecution.

Some readers may argue that Christians were persecuted in Roman lands. While this was true initially, remember that Christians later took over Rome and used its might to prohibit any other religion. Additionally, throughout the centuries when the Romans were polytheists, they never fought against other religions or denied other gods in any of their territories; on the contrary, they were somewhat willing to absorb other gods and traditions. The Egyptians in their turn absorbed some foreign gods as well. Even the Romans offered to Jewish people the option of including their God in the Roman pantheon, although the Jews refused this offer because it would have been completely against the commandments of the Abrahamic god.

An interesting question arises. Why did Romans not persecute Jews as they did to Christians? The reason was that Jewish people do not have the target of spreading their religion over the world; they are just required to conquer and rule the Canaan territory; this was why Romans expelled Jews from there.

But the Romans recognized the threat that monotheistic Christianity represented for them, as you can read in the New Testament Jesus teaching his followers to conquer the whole world for Christianity (read the excerpt above). The older Romans' fears were realized when Christianity became the official Roman religion and began exterminating the traditional Roman religion, and as consequence, their civilization.

The end of Roman and Egyptian polytheism was the beginning of centuries of terror, suffering, and human sacrifice in such an extent as the world has never seen in any other age.

Book I

The Ancient Egyptian Philosophy:

Mythology

Cosmogony

Cosmology

Religion

Ancient Egyptian Philosophy: One of the Most Reliable the World Has Ever Seen

Where did the Egyptian civilization, one of the most prosperous civilization of its age, mainly invest its wealth? Not in military power, if this had been the case, it would never have been conquered by the Persians, Greeks, Romans, and the Islamic Empire.

Ancient Egyptian Pharaohs did not seek to be a military power over the rest of the world. Rather, the goal of ancient Egyptian people was to achieve and maintain equilibrium within its environment and in its society, what they did for more than 3000 years, even in terms of military defense.

Only by the perspective of ancient Egyptians can we see and understand what is wrong with our modern world. In the next pages, I will attempt to change your monotheistic perspective, which you have unavoidably developed through a lifetime of exposure to the Abrahamic tradition, to that of an ancient Egyptian raised by polytheistic tradition. I will guide you on a journey into a completely different way of thinking and seeing the cosmos.

This way of thinking, i.e., the ancient Egyptian philosophy, was the reliable foundation that allowed the ancient Egyptians to build and maintain the longest lasting civilization the world has ever seen.

The first thing that you need to keep in mind is that the ancient Egyptian religion was neither a matter of faith nor did it come from revelations, similar to that in Abrahamic religions; the Egyptian religion was a result of philosophizing, and consequently, it was a *philosophy*.

Ancient Egyptian Mythology: The Source of their Philosophy

To understand how ancient Egyptians thought the universe had been created, i.e., their cosmogony, and how they believed the universe worked, i.e., their cosmology, we need to understand their mythology.

There were many plots within ancient Egyptian mythology. There are at least three reasons for this diversity of thought and accounts. First, the ancient Egyptian civilization developed for more than 3000 years, and any society change over this duration. The second is that they had freedom of thought so that diverse ideas and speculations could share the stage, and the third is that ancient Egyptian scholars, like modern philosophers, thought about the cosmos and came up with many different explanation of the reality.

Even though there are many stories in ancient Egyptian mythology, the essential cosmogony and cosmology are the same.

Studying this mythology, we learn that to an ancient Egyptian, everything in the universe, from natural phenomena to living beings to social phenomena including economic and political matters, was a manifestation of *divine power*.

It is important that we open our minds and try to understand how an ancient Egyptian would have looked at things because their way of thinking was so different from our modern approach that we are not otherwise able to understand their minds with modern eyes.

One good example that proves how differently they saw the world is their frequent depiction of sexual organs in art. When a modern person sees an ancient depiction of an erect penis or other sexual image, we are usually embarrassed, but an ancient Egyptian would have looked at such images as expressions of divine power because every part of our body was believed to be a materialization of a divine power. The atmosphere, earth, sun, winds, dawn, twilight, night, stars, order, chaos, and everything else was seen as the manifestation of some divine power.

Following this approach, ancient Egyptians observed the phenomena that surrounded them to understand what kinds of divine powers were being manifested and in what way they interacted with each other; thereafter, they created their mythologies, i.e., their stories about the deities and their interactions.

As an example, consider how an expert from each tradition would tell the story of a hurricane. When modern meteorologists explain a powerful hurricane, they always begin the story by telling about how the ocean temperature rose and how the winds and other conditions in the various levels of the atmosphere became favorable for the hurricane's development. Conversely, an ancient Egyptian would say that the God *Ocean* and Goddess *Atmosphere* engaged sexually and conceived the God *Hurricane*, their powerful divine offspring who is angry and destructive although short-lived, and then they would tell many other stories about this angry god and his power and deeds in relation to other gods such as the Earth, rivers, forests, and cities.

To learn about ancient Egyptian mythologies in more detail, you can read the beautiful book *Egyptian Mythology: A Guide to the Gods, Goddesses, and Tradition of Ancient Egypt* by Geraldine Pinch (Oxford University Press, 2002).

Ancient Egyptian Cosmogony

As challenging as it is for any civilization to make sense of everyday events, understanding the beginnings of the universe is almost excruciatingly difficult, even for modern people equipped with all of our scientific tools and developments. Despite this, the ancient Egyptians built a wonderful cosmogony in keeping with their down-to-earth way of thinking.

For them, in the beginning was the primeval water, the *oneness*; the meaning of this oneness for an ancient Egyptian was a single word: chaos. However, this chaos was full of potential for life. At that time, the universe was neither divided into the present diversity of things and beings nor were there pairs of opposite attributes such as male and female, darkness and light, life and death, cold and hot, void and full, earth and sky, wet and dry, positive and negative, and order and chaos. At that time, there existed solely the chaos full of life's potency.

Then the first god arose, the self-created one, whose name was Atum. Keep in mind that their gods' names had meaning, so that, when they said Atum, they thought "the self-created god."

Atum was also known as "the One Who Made Himself into Millions." This god, feeling his loneliness, decided to create many beings for accompaniment. Because procreation as we know requires sexual engagement between a male and a female, Atum, being the first individuality (in other words, consciousness) to emerge from the chaos, was believed to be both male and female simultaneously. This god masturbated, collected his own semen, and put it in his mouth, and when he wanted to create another god, he would spit some out and speak the name of the new creation. As we will discuss later, Ancient Egyptians believed that words have the divine power to change reality.

Every creation, according to their philosophy, requires three elements: the body, the divine essence, and the breath of life. The body is the form and substance of the creation; the divine essence comes from the divine will and thought that devised such creation; and the breath of life is the energy that animates the creation. In this sense, even inorganic things have "life," for every atom or particle has some energy and movement.

In this way, Atum, the first god, divided himself into the diverse things of the universe, including every living being. This god was believed to be the creator of all things after him, so he was the creator-god.

Ancient Egyptians understood the creation of the cosmos in this way because once they had realized that all things occur in pairs of opposites, as mentioned above, they concluded that the major force behind creation must also be a pair of opposites: chaos and order.

This explained why every creation is incessantly threatened by chaos and continually in danger of dissolving back into dust or oneness. Everyone can see the tendency of all things to return to chaos: we all know that every being dies and turns to dust and that every creation, even the mightiest buildings and machines, need to be continually cleaned and maintained or they will crumble into dust as well.

Because the opposite of chaos is order, with the creation of diversity, i.e., when Atum divided himself into millions and millions of things and beings, there arose the necessity to prevent these things and beings from returning to oneness, the need to restrain their inherent tendency to return to chaos. Thus, for his joy, Atum created the goddess *Ma'at*, the goddess of *truth*, *justice*, *order*, *harmony*, cosmic *beauty*, and cosmic *equilibrium*, who is responsible for manifesting the power that maintains order in the cosmos and that, in doing so, maintains the diversity that Atum has created.

For an ancient Egyptian, it was not possible to eliminate chaos, which was a divine force. In contemplating the phenomena of order and chaos, the ancient Egyptians thought that the creator-god Atum had endowed human beings with the power and given us the responsibility and choice to maintain Ma'at in the universe.

In contrast to some modern philosophies, it is interesting to note that ancient Egyptians did not see order as being hostile to diversity. According to their way of thinking, they knew that harmony among diverse elements is reached when we arrange diverse things in order. They knew that without order, the diversity of elements would fall into destruction and creation would return to chaos, to ash, to oneness.

In their view, order is vital to the maintenance of diversity. Without Ma'at, everything returns to chaos.

To grasp this ancient concept with our modern minds, it may help to compare the ancient Egyptians' deep respect for Ma'at with our enjoyment of a garden. A beautiful garden is characterized by both diversity and order, where we notice and appreciate its harmony, which we interpret as beauty. Furthermore, in art, the genius of the artist is the capacity to arrange the diversity of forms and colors to create beauty, wonder, sensation, and enchantment. If an artist were to mingle every form and color, the result would be oneness, or, in the word of an ancient Egyptian, chaos.

In short, they saw that diversity is intrinsically tied to order and vice-versa; it is not possible to reach order with equal things[1] and it is also not possible to nourish diversity without order.

The Life Cycle of Chaos and Order. The key to understanding the life cycle of chaos and order in ancient Egyptian cosmogony and cosmology is to know that chaos does not mean death; rather, chaos is the end of diversity. However, once a state of chaos has been reached, another cycle of creation and diversity can begin.

Thus, chaos contains the power of life in itself.

It is surprising that the ancient Egyptians understood this concept and architecture of reality so well more than 4,000 years ago simply through intensely observing their environment, without the knowledge of paleontology that allows us today to be aware that after each of Earth's five mass extinctions to date, creation is more diversified again.

No matter what happens, the power of life is insuperable, and no one can defeat Atum's will to create diversity: his determination to divide himself into millions of things and beings is insurmountable.

---

1.   If you get in hand some quantity of equal things and order them spatially, from this action, you presently created diversity through the different places you used to assemble them, and then they are no more absolutely equal.

Ancient Egyptian Cosmology

Now we will discuss how ancient Egyptians thought the universe worked.

For them, everything in the universe was a manifestation or an expression of divine power. There were no phenomena in either nature or society that did not spring from divine power as their source.

Today we look at things and phenomena and divide them into two types: earthly and transcendental (or spiritual if you will). For ancient Egyptians, in contrast, this kind of separation was not meaningful. Rather, every earthly phenomenon was an expression of a type of transcendental power. Therefore, they looked at the world from the perspective that everything in it had both physical and transcendental components!

This approach explains why, for them, there was no separation between religion and other spheres of life. To get an idea of how everything was thought to be immersed in the realm of religion, we must bear in mind that an ancient Egyptian would not have understood why this book is presently discussing religion as if it were a subject apart from everything else and as if it were an optional aspect to be include in our lives. Religion was not an option to them; it was perceived as the true reality of the cosmos.

But it is important for us to question: What does "transcendental" really mean?

The Meaning of "Transcendental"

It is necessary to explain why ancient Egyptians understood the world to be immersed in religion for you to comprehend that this perception is rather a down-to-earth approach than superstition.

Imagine that you not only like chocolate but also feel driven to find out *why* you like it.

The first answer to this question that a modern scientist would give is that your tongue has chemical receptors and that when stimulated with a particular chemical, these receptors unleash a chemical reaction in your brain that is responsible for your sensation of pleasure.

Then you might question the scientist and ask why you have such receptors and why they unleash that chain reaction from chocolate taste. Modern science would respond that these receptors and this reaction are encoded in your DNA. But why, you might press on, is our DNA encoded to create these things? Science answers that this is because it benefited your ancestors to enjoy certain tastes as it led them to seek more of the foods that helped them survive, perhaps citing some statistical figures about the likelihood that your inherited tastes are as they are. Yet there is always room for one more "why," and it will not be long until the scientist is forced to admit that she does not know the ultimate answer to these questions. Science can show that these phenomena exist, but it cannot answer the question of why our bodies function in particular ways.

Do you know about the placebo effect? An example of this powerful phenomenon occurs when someone takes a sugar pill containing no medication. If the person believes this pill to contain an effective drug, he or she may experience relief or healing although no medication has been delivered. What is the explanation for this?

In general, drugs must be more effective than a placebo to be approved for sale. However, consider that some genuine drugs can heal 70% of patients, while for the same illness, a placebo can heal up to 20%.

This leads us to wonder what portion of any cure is due to the active drug and what portion is due to the placebo effect. Surely the placebo effect, which is so powerful in people who take a sham drug, must also contribute to the cure in people who take the active drug. But this answer seems to be impossible to unravel.

Even doctors and researchers do not understand all of a drug's chemical mechanisms. Sometimes all they can guarantee is that, statistically, the drug is effective.

Regarding the placebo effect, why do scientists try to deny the transcendental aspect of this apparently unexplainable effect? Why do scientists dismiss this effect as "merely psychological"? Saying that this kind of effect is only in the mind does not erase the fact that there is some kind of power at work that can be used for human benefit.

Another interesting thing to consider is whether the power unleashed in the placebo effect occurs from inside or outside the person who experiences it. We may never understand this clearly.

As these examples have shown, scientific knowledge cannot explain everything. In fact, it cannot even explain certain questions that are directly related to biology and medicine. Given this, we cannot reasonably deny the existence of a power beyond the comprehension of science.

I want to mention one more interesting phenomenon that apparently cannot be explained through scientific thinking. Most people have heard about the "broken window theory" in criminology. This theory states that visible signs of crime, anti-social behavior, and civil disorder create an urban environment that encourages further crime and disorder. In other words, disorder unleashes disorder, whereas order unleashes order; bad behavior results in further bad behavior, and good behavior results in further good behavior.

Much research can be found on this subject. The reality is that the phenomenon is real, and the power behind it is real. Many of the criticisms of this theory, in fact, stem only from our inability to find the main material cause of this phenomenon; here, the social sciences have failed to explain what we can observe to be true. In terms of physical causation, there is no final explanation for this phenomenon, but the fact is real and undeniable.

These examples are meant to give you a sense of what it means for something in our world to be *transcendental*. Something that is transcendental is an *invisible* element, power, or phenomenon that we can observe but cannot explain by physical measurements alone.

These examples certainly demonstrate that transcendental elements exist, even though we do not understand them. No one can say that something does not exist simply because they do not understand why it exists.

Now that we have discussed ancient Egyptian cosmogony and cosmology as well as the existence and the meaning of the transcendental, we are equipped to dive into the ancient Egyptian religion.

The Ancient Egyptian Religion

Given all that we have discussed above, I think a good definition of religion is "the relation between human beings and the transcendental world."

In this sense, you can comprehend why, for an ancient Egyptian:

- Every human action needs a divine power to be executed, and
- Human beings can only employ transcendental power *through* the use of earthly elements.

Following this comprehension, while in modern times, we understand effective medications as mere chemical compounds, ancient Egyptians would have seen the release of some divine power by the drug as a mean.

Divine powers or gods? There is still an additional question to be answered: if we are talking about *divine powers*, why did they consider these divine powers as *beings* or *gods*, and not as impersonal powers occurring in nature? In other words, why did they believe that the natural powers of the universe had will, desire, and personality?

This tendency was an expression of their desire to have prudence and modesty in the face of the cosmos.

Even modern people often perceive some intention or mood to natural phenomena such as storms, natural disasters, and the law of physics. As we already know, we can always infer that something transcendental exists beyond everything we see in this world.

Rather than being superstitious, ancient Egyptians were *open-minded* regarding the existence of certain *beings* behind every phenomenon or power they encountered in their daily lives. It is not wise to deny the existence of something simply due to our inability to see it. Thus, they saw that everything on earth was some sort of divine power materialized, and although the objects and phenomena they saw on earth were not exactly gods themselves, each one somehow carried in itself the behavior of a god; in other words, the gods reveal themselves through the earthly manifestation of their powers.

From our modern perspective, which has been tailored through the presumption that only one god exists, it is natural to question why did the ancient Egyptians not simplify their religion by choosing only one god to worship? A good choice, we might think, would have been Atum as he was the creator of all things and the one from whom all powers emanated?

Because of the great diversity of things and beings on our planet, we can never see the true essence of the creator-god. Atum is hidden in the diversity of things and lives in the cosmos. The Egyptians saw that everything in the cosmos was distinct in its form, powers, and attributes. For example, animals with the power to fly exhibit distinct forms and attributes from all other kinds of animals. Even among birds, each species has different powers and attributes that come from the specific form wherein it was created. The ancient Egyptians observed that each thing has its own unique powers, characteristics, and attributes arising from the *special way* in which it was *crafted*.

Furthermore, they understood that mixing things with different characteristics results in another thing different from either of the original ingredients—a new creation. For example, wet is different from dry; if you mix them you get something damp, which is neither wet nor dry. Night is different from day; if you mix them you get neither night nor day but rather twilight or dawn. This is valid in all situations as you can prove to yourself through a few simple thought experiments.[2]

In this way, each kind of divine power manifests itself through different earthly elements or things.

---

2   Let's refer to the Periodic Table; every chemical element can be built using the same three basic substances—proton, neutron, and electron. It's astonishing that just combining a different number of protons, neutrons, and electrons can produce such distinct chemical elements, each one with its absolutely unique collection of characteristics.

The same theory can be composed with respect to chemical compounds as using the same amount of certain chemical elements, it is possible to produce different chemical compounds with completely different group of characteristics, powers, and attributes.

Therefore, we never see a manifestation of all divine powers together in a single earthly element.

In keeping with this truth, there is no medication that can cure all illnesses, there is no one animal that has all of the powers, attributes, and forms that an animal can have, and there is no single substance exhibiting all colors simultaneously or possessing all possible chemical characteristics at once.

Imagine mixing together all of the characteristics of all things that exist in the entire universe, not leaving a single thing out of the mixture, and imagine what you would get: chaos. No one has ever seen such chaos, and we do not even have an accurate idea of what it would be like.

In fact, the only being that can experience this chaos and survive is the creator-god Atum, who has the power of chaos in his *hands.* As for us, we can only see the things that were created by Atum, after him. We cannot *directly* see any earthly manifestation of Atum because to see Atum would be to see chaos itself, and we would not survive.

This is the reason why they called the creator-god Atum "the hidden one," which in their language was Amun; Atum and Amun are two names for the same god.

Recalling that creator-god Atum, "the One Who Made Himself into Millions," creates everything dividing himself into millions of things and in seeing that everything in the universe shows us its behavior, from the laws of physics, passing through things such as an atom, to the beings, they understood that in the transcendental world, whence everything comes from, to be out of chaos, Atum divided himself into different gods, powerful transcendental beings gifted with freedom of choice.

For ancient Egyptians the phenomena here on the material world reflect the phenomena in the transcendental world. For them there was no better and secure way to explain the transcendental world.

The ancient Egyptian cosmogony and cosmology are truly a marvelous philosophy to behold.

Ancient Egyptian Gods: Their Depictions and Earthly Manifestations

Let me be clear: the earthly manifestation of a transcendental truth is one thing, but the depiction of a god is another thing entirely.

This is easy to see with regard to the creator-god Atum/Amun. There are many depictions of the god Amun with the head of a ram because the main feature of Amun was his creative power, which the ancient Egyptians identified with the virility of rams. Because of these depictions, we could be tempted to think that the ram was regarded as the earthly manifestation of Atum, but it was not; remember that the god Atum was believed to be male and female at the same time, whereas beings on Earth are normally either male or female.

Accordingly, the ancient Egyptians depicted each god in different ways that made a statement about the specific powers that they recognized in that particular god, e.g., the Sun God Ra could manifest himself in 75 different forms. In total, they recognized around 1,500 gods.

The Afterlife: The Life That Never Ends

As you have seen, the ancient Egyptians were really *down-to-earth* in their approach to understanding the cosmos. Their approach to understanding the afterlife was no different.

Since everything needs to have a transcendental counterpart to be materialized on Earth, it follows that this also had to be the case with human life. As the afterlife is a highly speculative matter, the ancient Egyptians studied the happenings in this world to devise what must be occurring in the transcendental one. In doing so, they observed that the entire universe works in cycles of birth, death, and rebirth.

They saw the sun, a manifestation of the God Ra, being born in the East and crossing the sky, reaching his apogee at noon, then declining and dying in the West and finally entering the underworld at night, the domain of darkness and chaos. They understood the underworld as a threat to life, for they knew that, without sunlight, there could be no life on earth. Thus, for them, daylight and the sun represented good beings who were recognized for building things and nourishing their offspring, whereas the night was identified with unpleasant creatures lurking in the darkness to catch their prey. Therefore, the day was identified with life and the night with death.

When the sun god Ra entered into the darkness of the underworld, the earth entered into the darkness of night as well; as the Egyptians had to confront threatening beings in the night here on Earth, the sun god Ra must have been confronting comparable threatening beings in the underworld.

Remember that, for them, death was not the end of life but rather a return to chaos, from which the diversity of life will always emerge again. Therefore, after sunset, the sun god Ra was said to become "dead" because he was in the underworld fighting against the forces of chaos, but he always won the battle and was reborn as the same god Ra in the East.

For the ancient Egyptians, this cycle meant that just as we awaken in the morning and fall asleep at night, waking, and rising again when the sun god Ra rises the next morning, so it is in the rise and fall of our lives: in the beginning we are born, we achieve the peak of life at the middle of our time, and finally decline through old age until our "death," which signifies our entrance into the underworld, where we will confront the forces of chaos until our rebirth in the realm of the gods forever[3].

One of the first things that they believed would happen to each person entering the underworld was the weighing of the deceased's heart.

The judgment of the dead. Do you remember Ma'at, the goddess of truth, justice, order, harmony, cosmic beauty, and cosmic equilibrium? Upon entering the underworld, the heart of each person would be weighed against the feather of Ma'at to check whether the deceased had acted against the 42 commandments of Ma'at in life[4].

After the material body had died, the human soul would then be reborn in the transcendental realm of the gods. The afterlife is the phase of life wherein we live jointly with the gods. If you were a good person during your time on Earth, you would live in a pleasant place in the afterlife; if not, then you would live in a repulsive one. Certainly, the afterlife is and was a highly speculative subject, but the ancient Egyptians based their assumptions about it on what they saw in the world around them: they conjectured that a good person would live in a "field of reeds," which they would have described as a pleasant place, while a bad person would live in a swamp, which in Egypt was considered fetid and was full of crocodiles, hippos, snakes, and other dangerous animals.

Here is a good question: why did they take such care to preserve the corpses of the deceased through mummification and why did they go to such trouble and expense to build their wonderful tombs, such as the pyramids?

---

3   The ancient Egyptians believed that they could reincarnate on Earth again, but it was not a desirable happening; this was one of the reasons why they keep the corpse mummified so that they are not reborn on Earth.

4   Unlike the Ten Commandments of the Abrahamic religions, which are said to be "a revelation of God," the 42 commandments of Ma'at came from philosophers' reflections on how to maintain Ma'at in the world.

Of several reasons, only one reason is predominantly important for our book. If the body of the deceased was a manifestation on the earth of their soul and if the soul of the deceased was in the realm of the gods, preserving the corpse would enable the survivors to maintain an open link between the earth and the transcendental world. In this way, they believed that living people could contact the gods by means of their ancestors' corpses. They could then ask their ancestors to intervene with the gods on their behalf.

In the tombs, living people made offerings to the dead to make them happy as they would have done for them in life. This also ensured that the deceased would continue to help their descendants still living on Earth.

It is said that for as many centuries as the ancient Egyptians preserved the corpses of their deceased Pharaohs and made offerings and prayers to them, their civilization continued to prosper; when their religion changed and the cult of the deceased Pharaohs stopped, their civilization tumbled down as well.[5]

The belief that actions undertaken on earth using earthly elements could influence events in the transcendental world explains why the ancient polytheists made animal sacrifices as well. Because they recognized the presence of divine power manifested in flesh on Earth in the form of each animal's life, they used mummified animals' corpses to harness that divine power for their benefit. Millions of mummified animals have been found in excavations in Egypt, and ancient temples even raised animals for this purpose.

---

5   It is intriguing, to say the least, that the Catholic Church engages in almost the same practice as the ancient Egyptians did, embalming the popes for centuries to preserve their bodies and burying them in places that are just as grand and monumental as the Pharaohs' tombs were. Furthermore, the Catholic Church has continued to thrive throughout all the centuries during which they have followed this custom.

Pyramids and Temples: The Machine Built to Access the Gods' Realm

In short, divine powers can only manifest themselves on Earth through the use of earthly substances.

Temples, like pyramids, were the tools and access points through which the ancient Egyptians connected themselves to the gods. Each temple contained the image of a god for the same reason that each tomb contained a mummy. In front of some Pharaohs' tombs, there was even a temple for the worship of the Pharaoh who was buried in that tomb.

Unlike in many other philosophies, ancient Egyptians did not despise the physical body or the material world; the physical creation was not something to be defeated through puritanical efforts. Recall that, for them, transcendental powers could be employed through the use of earthly elements. Accordingly, they made use of everything that they recognized would be effective to contact and unleash divine powers for their benefit.

In this fashion, the temple's innermost part, where the god's statue was kept, was much more than *sacred*, as we think of religious places today; rather, the god's chamber **really was** an earthly manifestation of that god's transcendental dwelling, and the god's statue truly was a material manifestation of that god.

The secret chambers in ancient Egyptian temples represented the closest possible degree of access to the god's world for a human who was still living in the flesh.

The Sacred Rituals. For the ancient Egyptians, knowledge was power, and they believed that as they had more knowledge of how to access the gods than any other people, their civilization was supreme.

Before the priests entered a temple to complete a ritual, they performed rituals of purification with the expectation that they were truly about to enter into the god's transcendental world materialized on earth; once there, they expected to undergo a *transmutation* whereby the priests would become divinized so that they would be able to address the gods as if they were gods themselves. Once inside the innermost chamber, there was no other way to address the gods as they were in the gods' domain, which humans otherwise entered only in the afterlife. Outside of that chamber, however, the priests were not considered to be gods or even the gods' particular deputies.

This was the reason why, in contrast to modern houses of worship, the common people were granted practically no access to the temples and could never enter the ritual chambers.

Many rituals were performed every day, yet they were not put on as a show for people to watch. Rather, they were performed for the gods alone, to make them happy and to encourage them to help all people. Every element of each ritual was highly detailed, and the whole ritual was divided into many smaller ceremonies; below is a list of the ceremonies that made up the Morning Ritual that was executed every day in the Temple of Amun-Ra.

1. Utterance before the closed doors of the temple
2. Striking a Fire
3. Taking the Censer in the Hand
4. Placing the Incense on the Censer
5. Offering the Incense
6. The Invocation Hymn
7. Advancing to the Holy Place
8. Opening the Doors of the Shrine of the God
9. Looking Upon the God
10. Smelling the Earth
11. *Henu* Rite
12. Praying to the God
13. Offering the Heart to the God
14. Offering the Incense
15. Presenting Ma'at
16. The Festal Perfume in the Form of Honey
17. Laying the Hands on the God
18. Taking Off the God's Apparel
19. Purifications Made with the 4 White Vases
20. Purifications Made with the 4 Red Vases
21. Making the Purifications with Natron
22. The White Head Cloth

23. Putting on the White Head Cloth
24. Putting on the Green Head Cloth
25. Putting on the Red Head Cloth
26. Putting on the Great Cloth
27. Presenting the Unguent
28. Spell for Placing Myrrh on the Fire
29. Spell for Bringing the God to His Meal
30. Prayer of Praise
31. Scattering the Sand
32. The *Seman* Fragrance
33. Spell for Extinguishing the Candle
34. Spell for "Removing the Foot"
35. Concluding Utterance
36. The Reversion of Offerings

An important fact is that the food offerings presented to the gods were neither burned nor did the priests slaughter animals on the altar. The temple was sacred and the food was offered in cooked form, as we do normally; the last ceremony in each ritual was the ceremony of the Reversion of Offerings, during which some of the priests entered the temple again and retrieved the offered food so that it could be eaten by the priests and other employees of the temple.

But why do the gods need offerings?

The ancient Egyptians comprehend that, before they could ask one of the gods to manifest power on earth, they had to give the god some earthly substance to enable the god to engage with the physical world; in other words, just as food is what enables humans to sustain their lives in the flesh, so food would permit the gods to manifest themselves on earth in response to a prayer.

The Gods and the Common People. Commoners had access to the external parts of the temples where they could make their offerings and prayers to the gods. They could also order a prayer for their benefit from the priests, make offering, or buy an animal to be ritually mummified.

Furthermore, every home in ancient Egypt had its own shrine to the household's preferred gods and images of their ancestors to be worshiped.

The Power of Words and Forms. We have already explored how different transcendental elements took distinct forms when manifested physically (see the discussion above about the god Atum). One of the most powerful ways wherein transcendental realities can be manifest on earth is through the spoken and written word. With words alone a nation can make peace or enter into a war; words can even change the spirits of warriors such that a small outnumbered army becomes the strongest force; **only** through the *incorporeal, immaterial* and *untouchable* words can anyone of us think, invent, and access the knowledge that is immanent in the cosmos. They recognized the power that only words have to penetrate in the inaccessible parts of the human soul.

For the ancient Egyptians, therefore, without the spoken and written word there would have been nothing but chaos.

Recognizing the power of words in the material world, they reasoned that each word had a corresponding power in the transcendental realm. This is why their rituals were so detailed in terms of the forms and words that were used; this was also the reason why they believed that correct prayers would enable them to harness the gods' will and power for their benefit; even more than that, they believed that words have the power to change the reality, and their prayers reflect this perspective (later in the book you will have the opportunity to read a pyramid text where they used the words with this purpose).

They regarded the power of words and forms so highly that the ancient Egyptian language is one of the oldest written language in human history, with written records from 3,000 BCE. The advanced state and richness of ancient Egyptian literature from around 2,000 BCE is comparable to the classic literature of Europe, such as the writings of Shakespeare.

There were even some gods specific to the power of words and their written forms. The god of words, knowledge, and wisdom was Thoth or Djehuty, the goddess of the magical power of words was Heka, and the god of craft was Ptah.

There was, they believed, only one thing in the universe that was more powerful than ethereal words and forms: the creator-god Atum.

The Strongest Phenomenon in the Human Domain: The Social Power or the Power of the King

Recall how most of us feel and behave somewhat differently in the presence of an authority, such as your father, mother, or other older relatives; remember how you may have felt and acted when facing certain state authorities such as a deputy, senator, mayor, police officer, president, or judge. Think also about how you would feel in the presence of a successful businessperson, scientist, or priest. Most of us are likely to follow the commands of a person in authority and assume that their words are legitimate.

What then is the difference between an authority and those over whom they rule? How and why does this phenomenon, which I call "Social Power," materialize?

If the power of words is intangible, then Social Power is really *mystical* and *ethereal*. But this *magic* is invisibly executed in front of our eyes every single day.

Social Power manifests itself through the sum of the power of *words* and the power of *authority*.

I will dissect this mysterious but ever-present phenomenon by first scrutinizing a *related* phenomenon that astonishes people: hypnosis.

For the ancient Egyptians, hypnotism would have been viewed as a genuine manifestation of the divine power of the word combined with the divine power of authority.

Hypnosis is induced in four steps.

First step: The performer invites people to come together in a specific place. This is not necessarily a closed room; it can also be outside, even in a noisy environment.

Second step: The performer invites one or more people to be hypnotized from among those who are already gathered.

Third step: The performer begins to directly command those people to make certain movements according to his instructions. An important factor in this step is that the performer is touching his subjects.

Fourth step: When the performer is assured that those people are not resistant to his or her commands, he or she commands them to sleep.

The physical contact performed in the third and fourth step has two purposes. The first is to command specific movements and the second is to feel how willingly the people are obeying the commands. For example, the performer may ask you to give him your hand, then place it at some distance in front of your face, then command you to look at your palm and tell you that your hand is going toward your face, all the while touching the back of your palm softly with only one finger. This enables him to feel how completely you are accepting his commands. When he feels that you are already following him deeply, he commands you to sleep, and you will fall asleep.

The most important point to understand with regard to this phenomenon is that the "sleeping" is not the only part of the hypnosis process. Hypnosis truly begins when people first pay attention to the performer. Regardless of whether the first invitation was heard or read, the power of words is already working on the invited person; if a person believes in some degree that the performer can hypnotize people, the power of authority is materializing itself between the hypnotizer and invited person.

After this, the performer can produce and deepen different types and levels of hypnosis. Even people who deny that the performer has the power to hypnotize people still accept the authoritative power of the performer to some extent. Look at where the skeptics who deny the power of the performer usually position themselves: they typically stay and watch the performance anyway, along with the other people watching. If a person really did not believe in the power of the performer, he or she would not stay there watching and waiting to see what would happen. Even skeptics follow some of the commands given to them; hence, they are actually under the performer's authority as well.

The hypnotizer understands that the skeptics are placing themselves under the power of his authority. The skeptics are actually doing everything that the hypnotizer asks. In this way, we can observe skeptics being as thoroughly hypnotized as anyone else!

This phenomenon is a terrifying way to show how real the Social Power is and how it works. The power of authority manifests such that we cannot just say that people give the power of authority to someone or that the authority has that power. What we can say is that the power of authority manifests itself between the leader and the followers.

Hypnosis can neither occur if the hypnotist has no authority over the person nor if the hypnotist does not use words. Both authority and words need to be used to unleash that power.

A common error is thinking that hypnosis occurs only in the sleep state. This is not the case. In fact, we are constantly immersed in an environment of different types and levels of hypnosis!

Whenever you pay attention to something or someone, you are in a state of hypnosis. It does not matter if you are watching TV so intensely that you cannot hear someone else calling to you, or if you are paying attention to a sound or the thoughts in your own mind.

Even a simple request such as asking someone to pass you the salt can be a command that places the respondent under your authority or saying "Hi" to someone and expecting them to say "Hi" in response is pressuring them to obey the *command* of your greeting; therefore, every interaction between people is the manifestation of the power that can be called "hypnosis" or, perhaps more accurately, "Social Power" or the "Power of the King."

When you vote for a particular politician, you are experiencing this power over you. When you accept a command from someone else, you are in a state of hypnosis. When you pay attention to anyone, be it a priest, a lecturer, a professor, your parents, your siblings, even a salesperson, you are subjected to a type of hypnosis or Social Power.

This phenomenon explains why people *blindly* follow the commands of many kinds of leaders, even commands to sacrifice themselves in wars.

Pay attention to TV shows, advertisements, and financial scammers and notice how they use amazing techniques to exert Social Power over people. Some priests do the same thing.

One important thing that you need to know is that no one can hypnotize you without your consent: it is impossible. It is always possible for you to say "Hi" to someone and get no response, despite the strength with which is the "command of greeting."

The Ancient Egyptian Kingship

From all we discussed above, ancient Egyptian kingship also was considered to be a divine rule. The king was a deputy of the God Atum and he was required by Him to maintain Ma'at, the goddess of truth, justice, order, harmony, cosmic beauty, and cosmic equilibrium manifested on Earth.

An important distinction that the ancient Egyptians understood is that what is divine is the power of authority, not the person who embodies it. Hence, the king himself was not a divine manifestation of god; it was specifically the kingship that was regarded as an earthly manifestation of a divine power. For this reason, the ancient Egyptian kings were considered gods only after their deaths as anyone else.

Book II

Abrahamic Monotheism: A Theological Investigation

Judaism

Christianity

Islam

Vital Theological Questions

Now that we are deeply immersed in the ancient Near Eastern mentality, we are well equipped to deal with the three Abrahamic religions because we have the mindset of the polytheistic people among whom Judaism, Christianity, and Islam arose.

Most people in Western countries think that only one god exists in the universe and even claim that this belief is based on the Bible. This is a strange explanation, to say the least, because the Abrahamic texts in the Bible contain many contradictory passages. In fact, the Bible is full of phrases attesting the existence of many gods.

In Exodus 20, we can read the command that "You shall have no other gods but me."

As another example, take Deuteronomy 13:

> If your brother, the son of your mother, or your son or your daughter or the wife you embrace or your friend who is as your own soul entices you secretly, saying, 'Let us go and serve other gods,' which neither you nor your fathers have known, some of the gods of the peoples who are around you, whether near you or far off from you, from the one end of the earth to the other, you shall not yield to him or listen to him, nor shall your eye pity him, nor shall you spare him, nor shall you conceal him. But you shall kill him.

Clearly, it would be foolish to claim that the Bible teaches that there is only one god in the universe.

Another question is why people believe that the spiritual beings who have appeared to prophets are necessarily good beings. Even assuming that all prophets are telling the truth about what they have seen, we have only the words of the apparitions that they are in fact God's manifestations or messengers. Beyond that, why do people so readily accept the powers that these apparitions have shown to the prophets as sufficient evidence that they are in fact God or a God's messenger?

As we asked in the Preface[6], can we maintain that the prophets were wise or even of good judgment if they failed to question the truth of these messages when the apparitions told them that God wanted them to destroy other living beings, other parts of the creation?

One intrinsic and fundamental characteristic of the Abrahamic religions is that everything in their sacred scriptures is deemed to be a "revelation of God": their sacred texts "are God's words."

Yet when someone reports that he or she has seen God, or a messenger from God, this witness is taking it upon himself or herself to judge both the legitimacy and the good or bad nature of the apparition.

Furthermore, any listeners who trust in the witness's judgment and believe his or her story are likewise taking it upon themselves to judge the truth of these visions.

Such a self-centered response to a transcendental phenomenon is not only naïve and foolish but also imprudent, arrogant, and frightening.

In the previous section of this book, which dealt with the problem of seeing and contacting transcendental beings, recall how ancient Egyptians took a humbler and more down-to-earth approach in studying such phenomena.

For the ancient Egyptians, powerful beings such as gods in fact have enough power to manifest themselves to all people in everyday phenomena. The gods, after all, are the most powerful beings in

---

6   "If you are a powerful god and you are urging me to destroy some of the divine creation, I have only one thing to tell you: I myself am not great or powerful enough to judge whether you are really the creator of all things, or if you are even one of many gods with the power to create, nor can I judge if the power to manifest yourself like this is proof that you are a god at all. Therefore if you really are the all-powerful creator of all things and you desire to destroy something that you have created, or if you are some being authorized by the creator-god to destroy His creation, then you must go with your own awesome power and use it to destroy, kill, torture, and commit genocide by yourself. I will not do that on your behalf."

the cosmos with power to create all things in the universe and all kinds of life on Earth! What the gods have made themselves visible to one person, they have become visible to everyone else as well. Everyday natural phenomena are the true great miracles as they are available to be experienced by every living being. This truth can be summed up in the saying *"the sun rises for all."*

This is why ancient Egyptians, and possibly ancient people in general, believed that only minor spirits or weak beings such as demons would ever manifest themselves through hallucinatory visions or limit their manifestations to a few people at a time. The gods, in contrast, allow their manifestations to be seen by everyone who is willing to look.

Summing up, the questions we will investigate in this section are as follows:

1. Who judged whether each of the Biblical apparitions came from God?
2. Do the Abrahamic religions truly worship the creator-God, and is He the one who appeared to the prophets as recorded in the Bible?
3. In the end, who is responsible for the Bible's apparitions?
4. Can people consider the Biblical apparitions good beings?

A Theological Investigation of the Abrahamic Religions

As the three Abrahamic religions, Judaism, Christianity, and Islam, all have roots in the Jewish Bible, let's read some excerpts from the English Standard Version of the Bible to begin our examination and address those crucial theological questions above.

The Jewish Bible: The Roots of the Abrahamic Religions

First, I will show you three contradictory passages. I have emphasized certain parts with bold text to call your attention to the key segments.

Genesis 32:22–30

> *"The same night he arose and took his two wives, his two female servants, and his eleven children, and crossed the ford of the Jabbok.*
>
> *He took them and sent them across the stream, and everything else that he had.*
>
> *And **Jacob** was left **alone**. And a man wrestled with him until the breaking of the day.*
>
> *When the man saw that he did not prevail against Jacob, he touched his hip socket, and Jacob's hip was put out of joint as he wrestled with him.*
>
> *Then he said, 'Let me go, for the day has broken.' But Jacob said, 'I will not let you go unless **you bless** me.'*
>
> *And he said to him, 'What is your name?' And he said, 'Jacob.'*
>
> *Then he said, 'Your name shall no longer be called Jacob, but Israel, for you have striven with God and with men, and have prevailed.'*
>
> *Then Jacob asked him, 'Please tell me your name.' But he said, 'Why is it that you ask my name?' And there, he blessed him.*
>
> *So, Jacob called the name of the place Peniel, saying, 'For I have **seen God face to face,** and yet my life has been delivered.'"*

Why did Jacob conclude that the man who had appeared to fight him was God? Note that when this reportedly happened, Jacob was alone. This same pattern of God appearing to prophets when they are alone is repeated throughout the Bible.

Exodus 33:20

> "'I will cause all My goodness to pass in front of you,' the LORD replied, 'and I will proclaim My name—the LORD—before you. I will have mercy on whom I have mercy, and I will have compassion on whom I have compassion.' And He added, 'You **cannot see** My face, for **no one can see Me and live.'**"

> Here the apparition identifies himself as "the Lord" and claims that no one can see Him and live. Yet Jacob had seen Him and remained alive, although Jacob himself could hardly believe it.

Isaiah 6

Isaiah reported having visions in which God revealed things to him.

> "In the year that King Uzziah died, **I saw the Lord**, high and exalted, seated on a throne; and the train of his robe filled the temple. Above him were seraphim, each with six wings: With two wings, they covered their faces, with two they covered their feet, and with two they were flying. And they were calling to one another:

> 'Holy, holy, holy is the Lord Almighty;
> the whole earth is full of his glory.'

> At the sound of their voices, the doorposts and thresholds shook, and the temple was filled with smoke.

> 'Woe to me!' I cried. 'I am **ruined**! For I am a man of unclean lips, and I live among a people of unclean lips, and **my eyes have seen the King**, the **Lord Almighty**.'"

In many cases when God speaks to people, He says that no one can see His face, and that if anyone were to see His face, they would die. Nevertheless, this teaching is contradicted by the many stories wherein someone does in fact see God and does not die.

The question is who were they then seeing? Who was communicating with the prophets?

Let's look at other passages containing several different names used for addressing God, showing that the followers of this tradition were aware of the existence of many gods. This will clarify that the Abrahamic religion is monotheistic not in the sense that its followers believed that only one god existed, but rather in the sense that they worshiped *only one* god among many others.

Genesis 12

> *"Now the **Lord** said to Abram, 'Go from your country and your kindred and your father›s house to the land that I will show you. And I will make of you a great nation, and I will bless you and make your name great, so that you will be a blessing. I will bless those who bless you, and him who dishonors you I will curse, and in you, all the families of the earth shall be blessed.'"*

Why did the Lord (God) ask Abraham to abandon his family and country to find a new nation? Was this not done to remove Abraham from his birth culture, which worshiped many gods? If God were really the only god in the universe, why did Abraham have to leave?

We have already seen that Abraham was living in a polytheistic world. One of the reasons why the people believed in so many gods was that it was common for each family to have its own patron god. The two passages below show this clearly.

Genesis 12:29

> *"'It is in my power to do you harm. But the **God of your father** spoke to me last night, saying, 'Be careful not to say anything to Jacob, either good or bad.'"*

Genesis 43:23

> *"He replied, 'Peace to you, do not be afraid. **Your God** and **the God of your father** has put treasure in your sacks for you. I received your money.' Then he brought Simeon out to them."*

Below I will quote many other passages showing that for the followers of this tradition, there were many gods in the universe, yet one god among them was compelling them to become loyal to Him alone and to reject all other gods completely.

Genesis 35

> *"God said to Jacob, 'Arise, go up to Bethel and dwell there. Make an altar there to the God **who appeared** to you when you fled from your brother Esau.'*
>
> *So, Jacob said to his household and to all who were with him, '**Put away the foreign gods** that are among you and purify yourselves and change your garments.*
>
> *Then let us arise and go up to Bethel, so that I may make there an altar to **the God who** answers me in the day of my distress and has been with me wherever I have gone.'*
>
> *So, they gave to Jacob **all the foreign gods** that they had and the rings that were in their ears. Jacob hid them under the terebinth tree that was near Shechem."*

Genesis 48:15

> *"And he blessed Joseph and said,*
>
> *'**The God** before whom my fathers Abraham and Isaac walked, **the God** who has been my shepherd all my life long to this day, the angel who has redeemed me from all evil, bless the boys; and in them let my name be carried on, and the name of my fathers Abraham and Isaac; and let them grow into a multitude in the midst of the earth.'"*

Genesis 50:17

> *"'Say to Joseph, 'Please forgive the transgression of your brothers and their sin, because they did evil to you.' And now, please forgive the transgression of the servants of **the God of your father**.' Joseph wept when they spoke to him."*

Exodus 3:1–6

> *"And Moses said, 'I will turn aside to see this great sight, why the bush is not burned.' When the **Lord** saw that he turned aside to see, God called to him out of the bush, 'Moses, Moses!' And he said, 'Here I am.'*
>
> *Then he said, 'Do not come near; take your sandals off your feet, for the place on which you are standing is holy ground.'*

*And he said, 'I am **the God of your father**, the God **of Abraham**, the God **of Isaac**, and the God **of Jacob**.' And Moses hid his face, for he was afraid to look at God."*

Starting now, I will quote several Biblical passages wherein you need to note the following things:

1. Their god has specific names that differentiate him from other gods.
2. Their god asks for offerings.
3. Their god asks for animal and human sacrifices to placate his ire or in exchange for favors such as land and wealth.
4. Their god is vengeful.
5. Their god requires absolute loyalty.
6. Their god gives orders for them to eliminate all people who worship other gods, i.e., to engage in genocide.
7. Their god is very intolerant.

Exodus 13:12–16

"'Every firstborn of a donkey you shall redeem with a lamb, or if you will not redeem it you shall break its neck. Every firstborn of man among your sons you shall redeem.

And when in time to come your son asks you, 'What does this mean?' you shall say to him, 'By a strong hand the Lord brought us out of Egypt, from the house of slavery.

*For when Pharaoh stubbornly refused to let us go, the Lord **killed** all the firstborn in the land of Egypt, both the firstborn of **man** and the firstborn of **animals**. Therefore, **I sacrifice to the Lord** all the males that first open the womb, but all the firstborn of my sons I redeem.*

It shall be as a mark on your hand or frontlets between your eyes, for by a strong hand the Lord brought us out of Egypt.'"

Exodus 20:1–6

"And God spoke all these words, saying,

*'I am the **Lord your God**, who brought you out of the land of Egypt, out of the house of slavery.*

*You shall have **no other gods** before me.*

You shall not make for yourself a carved image, or any likeness of anything that is in heaven above, or that is in the earth beneath, or that is in the water under the earth.

*You shall not bow down to them or serve them, for I the Lord your God **am a jealous God**, visiting the iniquity of the fathers on the children to the third and the fourth generation of those who hate me, but showing steadfast love to thousands of those who love me and keep **my commandments**.'"*

Exodus 23:20–25

*"'Behold, I send an **angel** before you to guard you on the way and to bring you to the place that I have prepared.*

*Pay careful attention to him and obey his voice; do not rebel against him, for he will **not pardon your transgression**, for my name is in him.*

But if you carefully obey his voice and do all that I say, then I will be an enemy to your enemies and an adversary to your adversaries.

*When my angel goes before you and brings you to the Amorites and the Hittites and the Perizzites and the Canaanites, the Hivites and the Jebusites, and **I blot them out**, you shall not bow down to **their gods** nor serve them, nor do as they do, but you **shall utterly overthrow** them and break their pillars in pieces.*

*You shall serve the **Lord your God**, and he will bless your bread and your water, and I will take sickness away from among you.'"*

Exodus 32 (pay attention to my notes embedded in this quotation)

*"When the people saw that Moses delayed to come down from the mountain, the people gathered themselves together to Aaron and said to him, 'Up, **make us gods** who shall go before us. As for this Moses, the man who brought us up out of the land of Egypt, we do not know what has become of him.'*

So, Aaron said to them, 'Take off the rings of gold that are in the ears of your wives, your sons, and your daughters, and bring them to me.'

So, all the people took off the rings of gold that were in their ears and brought them to Aaron.

*And he received the gold from their hand and fashioned it with a graving tool and made a **golden calf**. And they said, '**These are your gods**, O Israel, who brought you up out of the land of Egypt!'*

*When Aaron saw this, he built an altar before it. And Aaron made a proclamation and said, 'Tomorrow shall be a **feast to the Lord**.' [Author's note: Here, "the Lord" refers to the god represented by the golden calf idol]*

And they rose up early the next day and offered burned offerings and brought peace offerings. And the people sat down to eat and drink and rose up to play.

*And the **Lord** said to Moses, 'Go down, for your people, whom you brought up out of the land of Egypt, have corrupted themselves.' [Here, "the Lord" refers to the God of Moses.]*

*They have turned aside quickly out of the way that I commanded them. They have made for themselves a golden calf and have worshiped it and **sacrificed** to it and said, 'These are **your gods**, O Israel, who brought you up out of the land of Egypt!'*

And the Lord said to Moses, 'I have seen this people, and behold, it is a stiff-necked people.

*Now therefore let me alone, that **my wrath** may burn hot against them and I may consume them, in order that I may make a great nation of you.'*

Exodus 32:27–29

*"And he said to them, 'Thus says the Lord God of Israel, 'Put your sword on your side each of you, and go to and from gate to gate throughout the camp, and each of you **kill his brother** and his **companion** and his **neighbor**.'*

*And the sons of Levi did according to the word of Moses. And that day about **three thousand men** of the people **fell**.*

*And Moses said, 'Today you have been ordained for the **service of the Lord**, each one at the cost of his son and of his brother, so that **He** might bestow a **blessing** upon you this day.'"*

So, they were blessed by the God of Israel after the offering of 3000 men as a human sacrifice for him.

Leviticus 1:1–9

> *"The **Lord** called Moses and spoke to him from the tent of meeting, saying,*
>
> *'Speak to the people of Israel and say to them, when any one of you brings an **offering to the Lord**, you shall bring your offering of **livestock** from the herd or from the flock.*
>
> *If his offering is a burned offering from the herd, he shall offer a male without blemish. He shall bring it to the entrance of the tent of meeting, that he may be accepted before the Lord.*
>
> *He shall lay his hand on the head of the burned offering, and it shall be accepted for him to make atonement for him.*
>
> *Then he shall **kill the bull before the Lord**, and Aaron's sons the priests shall bring the blood and throw the blood against the sides of the altar that is at the entrance of the tent of meeting. Then he shall flay the burned offering and cut it into pieces, and the sons of Aaron the priest shall put fire on the altar and arrange wood on the fire.*
>
> *And Aaron's sons the priests shall arrange the pieces, the head, and the fat, on the wood that is on the fire on the altar; but its entrails and its legs he shall wash with water. And the priest shall burn all of it on the altar, as a burned offering, a food offering with a pleasing aroma to the Lord.'"*

Numbers 14: 1 to 44

> *"Then all the congregation raised a loud cry, and the people wept that night. And all the people of Israel grumbled **against Moses** and Aaron.*
>
> *The whole congregation said to them, 'Would that we had died in the land of Egypt! Or would that we had died in this wilderness! **Why** is the Lord bringing us into this land, to fall by the sword? Our wives and our little ones will become a prey. Would it not be better for us to go back to Egypt?' And they said to one another, 'Let us choose a leader and go back to Egypt.'*

[Author's note: Their desire to return to Egypt suggests that they had been thriving there.]

*"Then Moses and Aaron fell on their faces before all the assembly of the congregation of the people of Israel. And Joshua the son of Nun and Caleb the son of Jephunneh, who were among those who had spied out the land, tore their clothes and said to all the congregation of the people of Israel, 'The land, which we passed through to spy it out, is an exceedingly good land. If the Lord delights in us, he will bring us into this land and give it to us, a land that flows with milk and honey. Only do not rebel against the Lord. And do not fear the **people** of the land, for they **are bread for us**. Their protection is removed from them, and **the Lord is with us**; do not fear them.' Then all the congregation said to stone them with stones. But the glory of the Lord appeared at the tent of meeting to all the people of Israel.*

*And the **Lord said** to Moses, 'How long will this people despise me? And how long will they not believe in me, in spite of all the signs that I have done among them? **I will strike them** with the **pestilence** and **disinherit** them, and I will make of you a nation greater and mightier than they.'*

But Moses said to the Lord, 'Then the Egyptians will hear of it, for you brought up this people in your might from among them, and they will tell the inhabitants of this land. They have heard that you, O Lord, are in the midst of this people. For you, O Lord, are seen face to face, and your cloud stands over them and you go before them, in a pillar of cloud by day and in a pillar of fire by night.

*Now if you **kill** this people as one man, then the nations who have heard your fame will say, 'It is because **the Lord was not able** to bring this people into the land that he swore to give to them that He has killed them in the wilderness.'*

*And now, **please let the power of the Lord be great as you have promised**, saying, 'The Lord is slow to anger and abounding in steadfast love, forgiving iniquity and transgression, but He will by no means clear the guilty, visiting the iniquity of the fathers on the children, to the third and the fourth generation.' Please pardon the iniquity of this people, according to the greatness of your steadfast love, just as you have forgiven this people, from Egypt until now.'"*

Then the Lord said, 'I have pardoned, according to your word. But truly, as I live, and as all the earth shall be filled with the glory of the Lord, none of the men who have seen my glory and my signs that I did in Egypt and in the wilderness, and yet have put me to the test these ten times and have not obeyed my voice, shall see the land that I swore to give to their fathers. And none of those who despised me shall see it. But my servant Caleb, because he has a different spirit and has followed me fully, I will bring into the land into which he went, and his descendants shall possess it. Now, since the Amalekites and the Canaanites dwell in the valleys, turn tomorrow and set out for the wilderness by the way to the Red Sea.'

And the Lord spoke to Moses and to Aaron, saying, 'How long shall this wicked congregation grumble against me? I have heard the grumblings of the people of Israel, which they grumble against me. Say to them, 'As I live, declares the Lord, what you have said in my hearing I will do to you: your dead bodies shall fall in this wilderness, and of all your number, listed in the census from twenty years old and upward, who have grumbled against me, not one shall come into the land where I swore that I would make you dwell, except Caleb the son of Jephunneh and Joshua the son of Nun. But your little ones, who you said would become a prey, I will bring in, and they shall know the land that you have rejected. But as for you, your dead bodies shall fall in this wilderness. And your children shall be shepherds in the wilderness forty years and shall suffer for your faithlessness, until the last of your dead bodies lies in the wilderness.

According to the number of the days in which you spied out the land, forty days, a year for each day, you shall bear your iniquity forty years, and you shall know my displeasure. I, the Lord, have spoken, surely this will I do to all this wicked congregation who are gathered together against me: in this wilderness they shall come to a full end, and there they shall die.'

And the men whom Moses sent to spy out the land, who returned and made all the congregation grumble against him by bringing up a bad report about the land— the men who brought up a bad report of the land—died by plague before the Lord. Of those men who went to spy out the land, only Joshua the son of Nun and Caleb the son of Jephunneh remained alive.

When Moses told these words to all the people of Israel, the people mourned greatly. And they rose early in the morning and went up to the heights of the hill country, saying, 'Here we are. We will go up to the place that the Lord has promised, for we have sinned.'

But Moses said, 'Why now are you transgressing the command of the Lord, when that will not succeed? Do not go up, for the **Lord is not among you,** *lest you be struck down before your enemies. For there the Amalekites and the Canaanites are facing you, and you shall fall by the sword. Because you have turned back from following the Lord, the Lord will not be with you.'*

But they presumed to go up to the heights of the hill country, although neither the ark of the covenant of the Lord nor Moses departed out of the camp. Then the Amalekites and the Canaanites who lived in that hill country came down and defeated them and pursued them, even to Hormah."

In the passage above and in the next, we can see that human sacrifice is required by this god to placate his ire.

Numbers 16:42–50

"And when the congregation had assembled against Moses and against Aaron, they turned toward the tent of meeting. And behold, the cloud covered it, and the glory of the Lord appeared. And Moses and Aaron came to the front of the tent of meeting, and **the Lord spoke** *to Moses, saying, 'Get away from the midst of this congregation, that* **I may consume them** *in a moment.'*

And they fell on their faces. And Moses said to Aaron, 'Take your censer, and put fire on it from off the altar and lay incense on it and carry it quickly to the congregation and make atonement for them, for wrath has gone out from the Lord; the plague has begun.' So, Aaron took it as Moses said and ran into the midst of the assembly. And behold, the plague had already begun among the people. And he put on the incense and made atonement for the people. And he stood between the dead and the living, and the plague was stopped. Now those who died in the plague were 14,700, besides those who died in the affair of Korah. And Aaron returned to Moses at the entrance of the tent of meeting, when the plague was stopped."

It is interesting that, in the passage above, Moses intervenes against God's will to save the people. In a choice between Moses and the god he follows, who is good and who is bad? Who is more powerful: Moses's god or the human beings who appear to have power over his behavior by burning incense? Who is this apparition which they believe to be a god?

Numbers 21:1–3

In this story, the Israelites clearly offer human sacrifice for the glory of their god.

> *"When the Canaanite, the king of Arad, who lived in the Negeb, heard that Israel was coming by the way of Atharim, he fought against Israel, and took some of them captive. And Israel vowed a vow to the Lord and said, 'If you will indeed give this people into my hand, then I will devote their cities to destruction.' And the Lord heeded the voice of Israel and gave over the Canaanites, and they devoted them and their cities to destruction. So, the name of the place was called Hormah."*

Numbers 21:34–35

Here we see another genocide commanded by their god.

> *"But the Lord said to Moses, 'Do not fear him, for I have given him into your hand, and all his people, and his land. And you shall do to him as you did to Sihon king of the Amorites, who lived at Heshbon.' So, they defeated him and his sons and all his people, until he had **no survivor left**. And they possessed his land."*

Numbers 25:1–5

Again, their god asks for human sacrifice to placate his ire.

> *"While Israel lived in Shittim, the people began to whore with the daughters of Moab. These invited the people to the sacrifices of **their gods**, and the people ate and bowed down to their gods. So, Israel yoked himself to Baal of Peor. And the **anger of the Lord** was kindled against Israel.*

And **the Lord said** to Moses, 'Take all the chiefs of the people and **hang them** in the sun before the Lord, that the fierce anger of the Lord may turn away from Israel.' And Moses said to the judges of Israel, 'Each of you kills those of his men who have yoked themselves to Baal of Peor.'"

Numbers 31:1–4

In this passage, their god asks for human sacrifice in revenge.

"The Lord spoke to Moses, saying, 'Avenge the people of Israel on the Midianites. Afterward, you shall be gathered to your people.' So, Moses spoke to the people, saying, 'Arm men from among you for the war, that they may go against Midian to **execute the Lord's vengeance** on Midian. You shall send a thousand from each of the tribes of Israel to the war.'"

Deuteronomy 1:6–8

Here their god commands them to take possession of certain land from other people.

"The Lord, our God, said to us in Horeb, 'You have stayed long enough at this mountain. Turn and take your journey, and go to the hill country of the Amorites and to all their neighbors in the Arabah, in the hill country and in the lowland and in the Negeb and by the seacoast, the land of the Canaanites, and Lebanon, as far as the great river, the river Euphrates. See, I have set the land before you. Go in and **take possession of the land** that the Lord swore to your fathers, to Abraham, to Isaac, and to Jacob, to give to them and to their offspring after them.'"

Deuteronomy 1:26–28

Observe what kind of god they believed their god to be and ask yourself how a leader would have to behave to evoke a similar response from his people.

"Yet you would not go up but rebelled against the command of **the Lord your God**. And you murmured in your tents and said, 'Because the Lord hated us, He has brought us out of the land of Egypt, to give us into the hand of the Amorites, **to**

destroy us. *Where are we going up? Our brothers have made our hearts melt, saying, 'The people are greater and taller than we. The cities are great and fortified up to heaven. And besides, we have seen the sons of the Anakim there.'"*

Deuteronomy 2:24–37

Here, another genocide (human sacrifice) is commanded by their god.

> *"The Lord said to me, '... Rise up, set out on your journey, and go over the Valley of the Arnon. Behold, I have given into your hand Sihon the Amorite, king of Heshbon, and his land. Begin to take possession and contend with him in battle. This day I will begin to put the dread and fear of you on the peoples who are under the whole heaven, who shall hear the report of you and shall tremble and be in anguish because of you.'*
>
> *So I sent messengers from the wilderness of Kedemoth to Sihon the king of Heshbon, with words of peace, saying, 'Let me pass through your land. I will go only by the road; I will turn aside neither to the right nor to the left. You shall sell me food for money, that I may eat, and give me water for money, that I may drink. Only let me pass through on foot, as the sons of Esau who live in Seir and the Moabites who live in Ar did for me until I go over the Jordan into the land that the Lord our God is giving to us.'*
>
> *But Sihon the king of Heshbon would not let us pass by him, for the Lord your God hardened his spirit and made his heart obstinate, that he might give him into your hand, as he is this day. And the Lord said to me, 'Behold, I have begun to give Sihon and his land over to you. Begin to take possession, that you may occupy his land.' Then Sihon came out against us, he and all his people, to battle at Jahaz. And the Lord our God gave him over to us, and we defeated him and his sons and all his people.* ***And we captured all his cities at that time and devoted to destruction every city, men, women, and children. We left no survivors.*** *Only the livestock we took as spoil for ourselves, with the plunder of the cities that we captured. From Aroer, which is on the edge of the Valley of the Arnon, and from the city that is in the valley, as far as Gilead, there was not a city too high for us. The Lord, our God, gave all into our hands. Only to the land*

of the sons of Ammon you did not draw near, that is, to all the banks of the river Jabbok and the cities of the hill country, whatever the Lord our God had forbidden us."

Deuteronomy 3:1–7

One more human sacrifice commanded by their god in such a scale that it only can be named genocide.

"Then we turned and went up the way to Bashan. And Og the king of Bashan came out against us, he and all his people, to battle at Edrei. But the Lord said to me, 'Do not fear him, for I have given him and all his people and his land into your hand. And you shall do to him as you did to Sihon the king of the Amorites, who lived at Heshbon.'

*So, the Lord our God gave into our hand Og also, the king of Bashan, and all his people, and we struck him down until he **had no survivor left**. And we took all his cities at that time— there was not a city that we did not take from them—**sixty cities**, the whole region of Argob, the kingdom of Og in Bashan. All these were cities fortified with high walls, gates, and bars, besides very many unwalled villages. And we devoted them to destruction, as we did to Sihon the king of Heshbon, devoting to destruction every city, men, women, and children. But all the livestock and the spoil of the cities **we took as our plunder**."*

Deuteronomy 4:1–4

Here, their god reaffirms that worshiping other gods will not be tolerated, and that all such infidels must be eliminated.

*"'And now, O Israel, listen to the statutes and the rules that I am teaching you, and do them, that you may live, and go in and **take possession of the land** that **the Lord,** the God of your fathers, is giving you.*

*You shall not add to the word that I command you, nor take from it, that you may keep the commandments of the Lord your God that I command you. Your eyes have seen what the Lord did at Baal-peor, for **the Lord your God destroyed** from among you all the men **who followed the Baal** of Peor. But you who held fast to the Lord your God are all alive today.'"*

Deuteronomy 7:1–6

Here we have more examples of human sacrifice including geno-cide, and more evidence of this god's intolerance, as well as a commandment that we will later discuss again, namely, to remain pure by not intermarrying with people who worship other gods.

It is important to note that at the end of this passage, this god reaf-firms that only the Israelites, among all the people on Earth, are His chosen people! We will discuss this later as well.

> *"'When the Lord, your God, brings you into the land that you are entering to take possession of it, and clears away many na-tions before you, the Hittites, the Girgashites, the Amorites, the Canaanites, the Perizzites, the Hivites, and the Jebusites, seven nations more numerous and mightier than you, and when the Lord, your God, gives them over to you, and you defeat them, then you must devote them to complete destruction.*

> *You shall make no covenant with them and show no mercy to them. You shall not intermarry with them, giving your daugh-ters to their sons or taking their daughters for your sons, for they would turn away your sons from following me, to serve other gods. Then the anger of the Lord would be kindled against you, and he would destroy you quickly. But thus, shall you deal with them: you shall break down their altars and dash in pieces their pillars and chop down their Asherim and burn their carved images with fire.*

> *For you are a people holy to the Lord your God. The Lord, your God, has chosen you to be a people for his treasured posses-sion, out of all the peoples who are on the face of the earth. It was not because you were more in number than any other people that the Lord set His love on you and chose you, for you were the fewest of all peoples...'"*

Deuteronomy 13:1–18

Again, we see the commandment to kill those who worship other gods, from an Israelite's own family to entire nations of strangers.

> *"If a prophet or a dreamer of dreams arises among you and gives you a sign or a wonder, and the sign or wonder that he*

tells you comes to pass, and if he says, 'Let us go after other gods,' which you have not known, 'and let us serve them,' you shall not listen to the words of that prophet or that dreamer of dreams. For the Lord, your God is testing you to know whether you love the Lord your God with all your heart and with all your soul. You shall walk after the Lord your God and fear him and keep his commandments and obey his voice, and you shall serve him and hold fast to him. But that prophet or that dreamer of dreams shall be put to death, because he has taught rebellion against the Lord your God, who brought you out of the land of Egypt and redeemed you out of the house of slavery, to make you leave the way in which the Lord your God commanded you to walk. So, you shall purge the evil from your midst.

*If your brother, the son of your mother, or your son or your daughter or the wife you embrace or your friend who is as your own soul entices you secretly, saying, 'Let us go and **serve other gods**,' which neither you nor your fathers have known, some of the **gods of the peoples** who are around you, whether near you or far off from you, from the one end of the earth to the other, you shall not yield to him or listen to him, nor shall your eye pity him, nor shall you spare him, nor shall you conceal him. But **you shall kill him**. Your hand shall be first against him to **put him to death,** and afterward the hand of all the people. You shall **stone him** to death with stones, because he sought to draw you away from the Lord your God, who brought you out of the land of Egypt, out of the house of slavery. And all Israel shall hear and fear and never again do any such wickedness as this among you.*

If you hear in one of your cities, which the Lord your God is giving you to dwell there, that certain worthless fellows have gone out among you and have drawn away the inhabitants of their city, saying, 'Let us go and serve other gods,' which you have not known, then you shall inquire and make search and ask diligently. And behold, if it be true and certain that such an abomination has been done among you, you shall surely put the inhabitants of that city to the sword, devoting it to destruction, all who are in it and its cattle, with the edge of the sword. You shall gather all its spoil into the midst of its open square and burn the city and all its spoil with fire, as a whole burned offering to the Lord your God. It shall be a heap forever. It shall not be built again. None of the devoted things shall stick to your hand, that the Lord may turn from the fierceness of his anger and show you mercy and have compassion on you and multiply you, as he swore to your fathers, if you obey the voice of the Lord your God, keeping all his commandments that I am commanding you today, and doing what is right in the sight of the Lord your God.'"

Isaiah 1:10–17

This prophetic writing features two key differences from the Torah excerpts above. First, their god is named differently: He is not called Lord but rather the God of hosts. Second, this God of hosts complains about the Israelite forms of worship, although God Himself prescribed these forms in the Torah texts.

Can these two transcendental entities be the same god?

"Hear, O heavens, and give ear, O earth;
  for the Lord has spoken:

'What to me is the multitude of your sacrifices?
  says the Lord;
I have had enough of burned offerings of rams
  and the fat of well-fed beasts;
I do not delight in the blood of bulls,
  or of lambs, or of goats.

When you come to appear before me,
  who has required of you
  this trampling of my courts?
Bring no more vain offerings;
  incense is an abomination to me.
New moon and Sabbath and the calling of convocations—
  I cannot endure iniquity and solemn assembly.
Your new moons and your appointed feasts
  my soul hates;
they have become a burden to me;
  I am weary of bearing them.
When you spread out your hands,
  I will hide my eyes from you;
even though you make many prayers,

> *I will not listen;*
>   *your hands are full of blood.*
> *Wash yourselves; make yourselves clean;*
>   *remove the evil of your deeds from before my eyes;*
> *cease to do evil,*
> *learn to do good;*
> *seek justice,*
>   *correct oppression;*
> *bring justice to the fatherless,*
>   *plead the widow's cause.'"*

In this divine speech recorded by Isaiah, the god who is speaking is so different from the god of the other excerpts from the Torah, He seems to be another god entirely. Not only here but throughout the Bible, God's behavior changes dramatically. Are there perhaps many different gods in the Bible, each competing for the total allegiance of the Israelites?

Although the Bible is full of texts that prove my point, I think that these excerpts are enough to demonstrate the pattern. Take your time to read the Bible without presuming anything about its god. Meanwhile, let's move on to accomplish our vital theological investigation.

Answering those Vital Theological Questions

Looking back at the questions to be answered:

1. Who judged whether each of the Biblical apparitions came from God?
2. Do the Abrahamic religions truly worship the creator-God, and is He the one who appeared to the prophets as recorded in the Bible?
3. In the end, who is responsible for the Bible's apparitions?
4. Can people consider the Biblical apparitions good beings?

Who determined that the apparitions had come from God?

This answer is the *key* that unlocks all the others.

Whenever a prophet reports seeing a vision of a god or of a god's messenger, the judge who assesses the truth of that apparition and its good or bad nature is not the god or the messenger but rather always the person who saw that vision.

Additionally, in making this assessment, the witness is also judging that he or she has the wisdom and authority enough to judge that the apparition was in fact a god and not any other kind of being. There is no way to escape from this fate—we are responsible for our assessments.

Furthermore, if people listen to the prophet and believe in his or her judgment, they are likewise acting as though they have the same wisdom and authority as the prophet. This excessive self-regard is also exhibited by anyone who declares that a particular writing is "the word of god" while some other document is not.

This behavior is not only naïve and foolish but also imprudent, arrogant, and worrisome because it allows people to avoid taking responsibility for their own actions. It allows anyone who claims to be following instructions received in a vision to act without conscience and to be free of guilt, shame, or remorse even if they have killed thousands of men, women, and children over ethnic or religious differences. Such heinous acts, combined with a total lack of guilt about them, is exactly what we see in history, repeated through the millennia, under the three Abrahamic religions.

The truth is that no living human has sufficient knowledge to affirm with no doubt that he or she has seen a god or a god's envoy. Yet the Abrahamic prophets and followers uniformly regarded themselves as sufficiently wise and capable to judge the nature of apparitions and even to identify the creator-God Himself.

Do the Abrahamic religions worship the creator-God? Is He the god who appeared to the prophets in the Bible?

The Abrahamic prophets never refuted the existence of other gods; they merely claimed that their god had chosen them from among all the other peoples on Earth.

On the contrary, from the beginning of the Bible, in Genesis 3, we can clearly see the authors' belief in the existence of many gods.

When Adam and Eve were living in the Garden of Eden, God told them never to eat the fruit from a specific tree in the garden, because if they ate it, He said, they would die. But a snake convinced Eve to eat that fruit saying:

> "'You will certainly not die,' the serpent said to the woman. 'For God knows that when you eat from it your eyes will be opened, and **you will be like God**, knowing good and evil.'"

And then, after they ate the fruits, the God said to them:

> "And **the Lord** God said, 'The man has now become like **one of us**, knowing good and evil. He must not be allowed to reach out his hand and take also from the tree of life and eat and live forever.'"

This god's awareness of other gods is unmistakable from the phrase "one of us." This use of "one of us" does not refer to any being living in the garden; rather, it is clear that the god is talking about other gods (don't miss the word "us"), because now that Adam and Eve have eaten the fruit and become "like God," they are not more like the any animal of creation; on the contrary, they are like divine beings, as the serpent had promised that they would be.

As we have read in the excerpts from the Jewish Bible, no one can be sure that the followers of the Abrahamic religions actually worship the creator-God because when Genesis was written, the Jewish people understood that other gods similar to their own existed. Indeed, their god was only one among many, a specific one who requires a name to distinguish Him: in some passages He is called the "God of your father," in others the "God of Israel," and in others the "God of hosts."

Thus, all that we have studied up to this point shows us that no one can be sure that it was in fact the creator-God who showed Himself to the Israelites and became their only god.

Who, then, was responsible for the apparitions that appeared to the Biblical prophets? Can we be certain that any of them were even good beings? These last two questions need to be answered together.

As their own accounts tell us, even the prophets were confused over the essence of the apparitions: they were baffled that they had apparently seen God and remained alive, when they believed, as they had been told, that anyone who saw God would die. Every time a prophet apparently saw God and yet did not die, this should have caused some mental alarm bells to ring; unfortunately, however, they overlooked this discrepancy.

Moreover, we can use the following fundamental theological thinking to answer the two questions together.

As we have already mentioned, anyone who is apparently commanded by God to kill other human beings and thereby destroy irreplaceable parts of the creation *must* question this command and attempt to find out where this most un-God-like message is really coming from.

Furthermore, any sensible person receiving such a vision should ask himself, if the gods are powerful enough to manifest their powers in the forms of the sun and other stars, as well as in every kind of life on Earth and every kind of material in the universe, why would a god appear to me alone? Wouldn't a real god have the power to appear to everyone at once, rather than relying on a single imperfect human to deliver the message to all the rest?

These questions are mandatory if we have any sense of our own humility or proper assessment of our own limited ability to judge the essence of an apparition. Instead of asking these prudent and modest questions, however, the Biblical "prophets" assumed that they were wise enough to judge these apparitions and determine that they were from the creator-God.

It is interesting to note that people apparently regard brief and flashy smoke-and-thunder apparitions such as those reported in the Bible as more true and meaningful than the visible manifestations of the creator-God' power that any of us can see every day, namely, His choices and His power as revealed through His invention and creation of every kind of life and every element in the universe. The creator-God has the power to create and infuse energy and life into billions and billions of stars, planets, solar systems, and galaxies and to create an incalculable variety of natural phenomena. Even so, most people judge that a vulgar apparition to one "prophet" contains more useful information, meaning, and power than all the rest of creation!

Furthermore, keeping in mind that the prophets knew that many gods did exist, they should certainly have asked the following important questions as well:

"Why among all the gods did you and only you choose us? And why did you choose us from among all the people on Earth to kill others and seize their lands? Why set yourself against the other gods and their people? Why do you want to eliminate their worship and their devotees from the Earth?"

Some may argue that, if the gods have the power to create anything they desire, then they must also have the power to appear as in the Biblical apparitions. Certainly, the gods do have that ability. But this does not excuse us from the responsibility of questioning the true origin of such visions.

No one can be called "wise" if they are not prudent enough to think of the critical theological questions above.

After all of these questions have been thought of and posed, any reasonable witness to an apparition would tell the apparition:

"As you know, I am not wise or powerful enough to judge for sure whether you are a god or a demon. So if you want to destroy some of God's creation, take the responsibility and do it yourself. I cannot do it on your behalf."

Although none of the Abrahamic prophets thought of these critical reflections at the time, this fact does not stop us from asking them now. From the evidence, we can reach the following conclusions:

1. This being who appeared to the Biblical prophets is weaker than other gods as he lacks the power to appear as anything more than a brief apparition.
2. This being used Social Power, i.e., the power of presumed authority and of words, to make people obey his command.
3. This being used the people he appeared to, *the chosen ones*, to commit terrible crimes such as plunder and genocide (or in other words, human sacrifice) for him and on his behalf.
4. Therefore, the Abrahamic "*god*" is actually a demon.

Now we can ask who is worse: this demon who asked people to commit genocide and kill innocents, or the people who actually put his commands into practice and are therefore truly responsible for those acts?

How the Wicked Abrahamic Demon Prevailed

Obviously there are many good and respectable aspects of the Abrahamic sacred texts, especially in the wisdom teachings. This is to be expected given that if the demon had spread lies and wickedness only or had commanded all of the Israelites to kill each other in a few years, his influence would soon vanish when there was no one left alive for him to command. No, it was more effective for the demon to mix some truth into his lies and wickedness so that the people he had enslaved would survive and continue to follow him.

Is there a more effective way to spread evil actions on Earth than convincing people that they are doing the right in God's sight, that they are guided by a wise being who knows what is best for the world, and that they will be blessed by this being if they follow his commands without listening to their own consciences?

In spite of all of his beautiful promises and true wisdom, however, the Abrahamic demon always kept the Jews in fear of his ire, as he frequently commanded them to fall on each other and kill the dissidents among them. Never forget this.

By all these means, the Abrahamic demon convinced the Israelites to make a covenant with him, a promise sealed in blood. After that, the Jewish people committed many human sacrifices and genocides as acts of worship for that demon.

Judaism: "The chosen ones"

Since we have already explored the Jewish Bible as the source of the Abrahamic traditions, there is little left to say of Judaism specifically.

The Jews believe that they are the chosen ones, specially selected by their *God* to be His own people.

Being devoted to the scriptures, Jews are required to follow their god's rules concerning clothes, food, marriage, and many other lifestyle details, as anyone can read in the Bible's Old Testament.

The idea that worship only comprises attending worship services is completely mistaken. Worship runs through every aspect of life, not only in the externally visible elements such as particular clothes and habits, but also in social phenomena such as the directive to socialize and associate as little as possible with non-Jewish people. Not only marriage to a non-Jew but even sitting down to a meal with one is prohibited by Jewish sacred scriptures.

Therefore, one might wonder why Jewish people do not attempt to kill non-Jewish people all over the world to conquer their lands or force their conversion to Judaism. This is because the Abrahamic demon compelled them to conquer ancient Canaan or modern Israel only. If any Jew must live outside of that region, the demon's commandment is to keep themselves isolated and pure as a people and to come back to the "promised land" someday.

In the Jewish scriptures, this demon never compels the Jews to convert outsiders, although he does require them to eliminate non-Jews from the promised land.

The mission to convert outsiders and to spread the demon's dominion to other lands would be a task for Christianity and Islam.

Christianity: The Abrahamic Empire

Like every other Abrahamic prophet, Jesus Christ claimed that he was in contact with the "God of Israel."

Jesus went further than the other prophets, however, when he claimed to somehow be the "God of Israel" on Earth, as we can read in the quotations below and throughout the New Testament.

John 14

> "'Let not your hearts be troubled. **Believe in God**; also **believe in me**. In my Father's house are many rooms. If it were not so, would I have told you that I go to prepare a place for you? And if I go and prepare a place for you, I will come again and will take you to myself, that where I am you may be also. And you know the way to where I am going.'
>
> Thomas said to him, '**Lord**, we do not know where you are going. How can we know the way?'
>
> Jesus said to him, '**I am the way**, and the **truth**, and the **life. No one comes to the Father except through me**. If you had known me, you would have known my Father also. From now on, you do know him and have **seen** him.'"

Matthew 5:17–20

> "'Do not think that I have come to abolish the Law or the Prophets; I have **not** come **to abolish** them but to fulfill them.
>
> For truly, I say to you, until heaven and earth pass away, **not an iota, not a dot,** will pass from the Law until **all is accomplished**. Therefore, whoever relaxes one of the least of these commandments and teaches others to do the same will be called least in the kingdom of heaven, but whoever does them and teaches them will be called great in the kingdom of heaven. For I tell you unless your righteousness exceeds that of the scribes and Pharisees, you will never enter the kingdom of heaven.'"

If this is not enough, we can also examine Matthew 28:

> "Then Jesus came to them and said, '**All authority** in **heaven** and on **earth** has been given to me. Therefore, go and make

*disciples of **all nations**, baptizing them in the name of the Father and of the Son and of the Holy Spirit, and teaching them to **obey everything** I have commanded you. And surely I am with you always, to the very end of the age.'"*

Here, we have the same pattern of threats that we see throughout the Bible: either you are loyal to me or you will be punished.

Additionally, Jesus tells his followers that the Law of the God of Israel will remain valid throughout the world and through all time.

What do you think Jesus was demanding of them when he said, *"For I tell you unless your righteousness exceeds that of the scribes and Pharisees, you will never enter the kingdom of heaven"*? What did he mean by "righteousness" in that phrase? Nothing less than to follow the orders of the "God of Israel."

Below, I quote Jesus's Sermon on the Mount. In the teachings of Jesus conveyed here, as in the other Abrahamic religions, the speaker attempts to encourage his followers by assuring them that the bad effects of their obedience to his commands are in fact positive outcomes.

Jesus says that he is fulfilling the Law of Abraham at the same time that he is teaching them a new thing, to engage in self-sacrifice, the most important innovation of the Abrahamic demon with Christianity. Pay attention to this teaching as we will further analyze it later.

Matthew 5

> *"Seeing the crowds, he went up on the mountain, and when he sat down, his disciples came to him.*
>
> *And he opened his mouth and taught them, saying:*
>
> *'Blessed are the poor in spirit, for theirs is the kingdom of heaven.*
>
> *Blessed are those who mourn, for they shall be comforted.*
>
> *Blessed are the meek, for they shall inherit the earth.*
>
> *Blessed are those who hunger and thirst for righteousness, for they shall be satisfied.*

Blessed are the merciful, for they shall receive mercy.

Blessed are the pure in heart, for they shall see God.

Blessed are the peacemakers, for they shall be called sons of God.

*Blessed are those **who are persecuted** for righteousness' sake, for theirs is the kingdom of heaven.*

*Blessed are you when **others revile you** and **persecute you** and utter all kinds of **evil against you** falsely on my account. **Rejoice** and be **glad**, for your reward is great in heaven, for so they persecuted the prophets who were before you.*

You are the salt of the earth, but if salt has lost its taste, how shall its saltiness be restored? It is no longer good for anything except to be thrown out and trampled under people's feet.

You are the light of the world. A city set on a hill cannot be hidden. Nor do people light a lamp and put it under a basket, but on a stand, and it gives light to all in the house. In the same way, let your light shine before others, so that they may see your good works and give glory to your Father who is in heaven.

Do not think that I have come to abolish the Law or the Prophets; I have not come to abolish them but to fulfill them. For truly, I say to you, until heaven and earth pass away, not an iota, not a dot, will pass from the Law until all is accomplished. Therefore, whoever relaxes one of the least of these commandments and teaches others to do the same will be called least in the kingdom of heaven, but whoever does them and teaches them will be called great in the kingdom of heaven. For I tell you, unless your righteousness exceeds that of the scribes and Pharisees, you will never enter the kingdom of heaven.

You have heard that it was said to those of old, 'You shall not murder; and whoever murders will be liable to judgment.' But I say to you that everyone who is angry with his brother will be liable to judgment; whoever insults his brother will be liable to the council; and whoever says, 'You fool!' will be liable to the hell of fire. So, if you are offering your gift at the altar and there remember that your brother has something against you, leave your gift there before the altar and go. First be reconciled to your brother, and then come and offer your gift. Come to terms quickly with your accuser while you are going with him to court, lest your accuser hand you over to the judge, and the judge to the guard, and you be put in prison. Truly, I say to you, you will never get out until you have paid the last penny.

You have heard that it was said, 'You shall not commit adultery.' But I say to you that everyone who looks at a woman with lustful intent has already committed adultery with her in his heart. If your right eye causes you to sin, tear it out and throw it away. For it is better that you lose one of your members than that your whole body be thrown into hell. And if your right hand causes you to sin, cut it off and throw it away. For it is better that you lose one of your members than that your whole body go into hell.

It was also said, 'Whoever divorces his wife, let him give her a certificate of divorce.' But I say to you that everyone who divorces his wife, except on the ground of sexual immorality, makes her commit adultery, and whoever marries a divorced woman commits adultery.

Again, you have heard that it was said to those of old, 'You shall not swear falsely, but shall perform to the Lord what you have sworn.' But I say to you, Do not take an oath at all, either by heaven, for it is the throne of God, or by the earth, for it is his footstool, or by Jerusalem, for it is the city of the great King. And do not take an oath by your head, for you cannot make one hair white or black. Let what you say be simply 'Yes' or 'No'; anything more than this comes from evil.

*You have heard that it was said, 'An eye for an eye and a tooth for a tooth.' But I say to you, **do not resist** the one who is **evil**. But if anyone **slaps you** on the right cheek, turn to him the other also. And if anyone would sue you and take your tunic, **let him have your cloak** as well. And if anyone forces you to go one mile, **go with him two miles.** Give to the one who begs from you, and do not refuse the one who would borrow from you.*

*You have heard that it was said, 'You shall love your neighbor and hate your enemy.' But I say to you, **love your enemies** and pray for those who persecute you, so that you may be sons of your Father who is in heaven. For he makes his sun rise on* *the evil and on the good and sends rain on the just and on the unjust. For if you love those who love you, what reward do you have? Do not even the tax collectors do the same? And if you greet only your brothers, what more are you doing than others? Do not even the Gentiles do the same? You therefore **must be perfect, as** your heavenly **Father is perfect.**'"*

This speech follows the old pattern of mixing good advice and wise commandments with bad advice to confuse and cheat people. In these verses, Jesus commands self-sacrifice. He commands his followers to love their enemies and to enslave themselves to evil people without regard for their own needs and safety:

"But if anyone slaps you on the right cheek, turn to him the other also. And if anyone would sue you and take your tunic, let him have your cloak as well. And if anyone forces you to go one mile, go with him two miles."

You can clearly see the commandment of self-sacrifice! Jesus confuses the people by using the word "love" to mean self-sacrifice. And Jesus was the first to put this new interpretation of love into practice. Why did Jesus command his followers to engage in self-sacrifice? What was the purpose of this?

The Abrahamic demon had a new, a huge, and terrifying goal: to build an Abrahamic Empire.

Warriors in an army need to be willing, and eager, to sacrifice themselves at any time. No army can win if its soldiers fear death. To achieve this, the demon used Jesus Christ's charisma and his own example of self-sacrifice to establish the necessary Social Power over people to put them under his command.

To achieve it his first recruit was Jesus Christ, who was also his general in this task and who recruited warriors to build a religious army as we saw it happening over centuries.

Social Power, the strongest phenomenon experienced by humans, is the power without which there is no kingship; it is the sum of the singular power of words and the insurmountable power of authority.

How did the Abrahamic demon achieve this power and sway the people to his side? By making Jesus able to perform "miracles." Remember that Jesus told his people, *"If you had known me, you would have known my Father also."* People who saw Jesus executing "miracles" therefore believed that they had seen the work of "God" with their own eyes! In this way, the demon manifested the power of authority over people through Jesus, so that, subsequently, Jesus simply had to use the power of words to command the people to do whatever the demon wanted.

In this way, the Abrahamic demon's reign of misery was established in the world and has lasted for generations. This demon has no strength to manifest himself on Earth, as a true god does, to achieve his goals, but he was clever enough to use trickery to force humans to materialize his wishes on Earth.

Sadly, like the other Abrahamic prophets, Jesus Christ did not exhibit enough intelligence, prudence and modesty to ask the vital theological questions we studied before. Thus, he fell under the sway of the villainous demon. Jesus did not recognize his fatal error until it was too late.

The God of Israel: The *God* of Deception, the *God* of Human Sacrifice

Throughout the Abrahamic peoples' history we can clearly see the same horrible thing happening again and again: the Abrahamic demon's devotees hurt other people and suffer themselves as well.

The proof that Jesus was cheated by this demon is the fact that, when he was about to die on the cross, he recognized it himself:

"And about the ninth hour Jesus cried out with a loud voice, saying, 'Eli, Eli, lema sabachthani?' that is, 'My God, my God, why have you forsaken me?' (Matthew 26:46)

But he was so convinced (or hypnotized?) that the demon was the God that he cried still calling the demon God.

However, by then, it was too late for him, for Christians and too late for humanity: the demon's goal had been accomplished!

You can see the same result when you read about Joan of Arc. She reported having visions of the archangel Michael, Saint Margaret, and Saint Catherine of Alexandria. She said that they had the power to predict decades' worth of events, which would suggest, of course, that they could also foresee the fate of Joan of Arc. Yet the apparitions never told her in advance that she would be sacrificed by being burned at the stake by her own beloved Catholic Church!

In the last month of her captivity the apparitions even told her that she would be freed, and this news made her happy. When she saw that she was in fact not going to escape, she became devastated. Reading the accounts of Joan of Arc, you can clearly imagine that she must have felt the same sense of betrayal as Jesus, the sense of abandonment by her *God* and his envoys.[7]

This demon always does the same thing to his servants and mouth-pieces on Earth, causing them to be sacrificed and leaving them to suffer the worst death possible once their work on his behalf is done.

---

7   You can read her miserable story in Twain, Mark. *Joan of Arc.* Ignatius Press, 2007. The author considered this book to be his best.

Likewise, where was the so powerful and full of miracles God of Israel to save Jews in the Nazi detention camps. Their *God* had abandoned them in the same way. What they did not understand is that their *god*, the demon they affectionately called the God of Israel, was in fact working to obtain human sacrifice, including that of his own followers.

The Theology of Miracles: Why Would a God Need to Perform *Miracles*?

We have already established that no one has enough wisdom to be certain that he or she has seen a god or a god's envoy as opposed to a demon or the spirit of a deceased person.

But what about miracles or paranormal deeds? Can anyone be sure that miracles are the acts of a god? Even if it can be proved that a miracle was in fact paranormal, how can people be sure that it came from a god? Why do people never seem to consider that it could have come from a demon?

Unfortunately, as we have seen among the ancient prophets with their apparitions, modern people including scholars assume that they have enough wisdom to know for certain that any miracles they might witness or hear about come from god as opposed to a demon or another entity.

It is curious that people are so confident in claiming that, just because Jesus performed miracles, he must have been animated by God's powerful *will*, when we never seem to question why Jesus, if he was an envoy of God, needed to perform *miracles* at all. Why show off his paranormal power? What was the purpose of his walking on water? What good did that do other than impressing his friends to mesmerize them?

"He expelled demons from people," one might say. Yes, but perhaps that was part of a setup so that he would not seem to be a demon, so that no one would question whether he was under a demon's commands.

"He healed people," one might say. Yes, but he also established the blood covenant by which his followers were bound to satisfy his god through their own self-sacrifice. He saved the lives of several dozen people so that the demon could swallow the blood of millions more throughout the centuries-long reign of monotheism. In what better way could a demon convince people of his goodness?

It is true that Jesus fulfilled the law promulgated by the God of Israel, but this law was the law of a demon.

The only purpose of Jesus's showy miracles was to secure Social Power over the people and convince them to enter into a bloody covenant with the demon they called the "God of Israel." Do you think that the creator-God, who created the entire universe and all physical phenomena, needs to show off this kind of power? Behold the cosmos, is the creation of the entire universe not enough of a miracle already, the most powerful one?

As we have discussed, genuine gods beyond doubt have enough power to manifest themselves to all people through everyday phenomena, whereas other transcendental beings, such as demons or deceased people, are limited to rare, weak, and ephemeral displays of power, even if they are exciting in some way.

One fundamental characteristic shared by all of the "miraculous" phenomena that people ascribe to the gods is that they are few in number and cannot be replicated on demand. The fact that a miracle is not replicable does not in any way prove that it was not a transcendental event; it suggests that the being who produced the miracle is a weak being, nowhere near as strong as a god! If this being were as powerful as a god, it would be able to produce endlessly replicable miracles, like those that the gods produce, namely, the everyday phenomena that sustain our lives, the lasting, perennial, universal cosmic experiences.

A great example of this can be found in "miracles" of healing. It is striking to note that an isolated "healing miracle" that heals one person in a way that science cannot explain is often said to be an act of a god, whereas the work of a researcher who develops a medicine that cures thousands or even millions of people every year for decades goes unremarked. Which has a more powerful effect: the one-time mystery recovery or the drug researcher's breakthrough? Surely the drug researcher has a greater impact on the world than a miracle worker who cures a few people with flashy magic. If we can accept that the drug researcher is not a god, it should be easy to refuse the statement that the miracle's healing comes from a god's deed either.

Note that although the drug researcher works through science, they are however using a god's power. The drug researcher has truly discovered an earthly manifestation of a divine power, and since this divine power legitimately comes from a god, it is naturally available to everyone to discover it, as are all manifestations of a genuine god! Can you grasp the huge difference between a divine manifestation and a demonic one?

It is sad to recognize, in our heightened regard for one-time miracles and our corresponding disregard for everyday miracles, the widespread assumption that the gods are weak beings who can only appear in our world for brief moments. It is nauseating to know that the gods, the most powerful beings in the cosmos, with the strength to create everything in this immeasurable universe, including all the interlocking laws of nature, are overlooked in favor of the clever but ultimately weaker demonic beings. How blind people have been to the gods, their powers, and their creation.

Self-Sacrifice: The Apex of Human Sacrifice

In the Sermon on the Mount, Jesus says that he came to fulfill the Law, i.e., the commandments that the God of Israel had revealed to the earlier Abrahamic prophets. He proclaimed that people needed to make a covenant with that god and only with him and that the only way to reach their god was through following Jesus, in other words, through obeying his commands of self-sacrifice.

How can anyone fulfill commandments that simultaneously encourage intolerance, hatred, and genocide as well as self-sacrifice for the enemies? What comes from this? Confusion!

This confusion arises both within a person's mind and among people. It explains a lot of what we see throughout the history of Christendom. This confusion is so deep that over the years Christianity itself has split into many branches due to the impossibility of being sure about how to accomplish the tasks required by the God of Israel. In this process, of course, the God of Israel is getting what he really wants: hatred, intolerance, and even literal human sacrifice and bloodshed in the many religious wars we have waged.

The typical pattern in Christendom is that good-hearted people who make a blood covenant with Jesus and his God and attempt to engage in self-sacrifice end up being dominated by evil people who follow the first part of the Abrahamic scriptures, the part commanding genocides.

Truly, the Abrahamic demon used Jesus to open the door to the domination of evil over every aspect of daily human life. Even noble self-denial can be unhealthy, as in the case of an abused wife. The churches has taught women in that situation that to obey the Sermon on the Mount, they should let their husbands abuse them as they will then be blessed for their self-sacrifice and for loving their enemies.

This is a classic example of what has happened over the centuries since Jesus's teaching has spread. Do you want to find corruption, abusers, perverse criminals? Look in the churches, especially where the church closely works with governments.

Only good-hearted and naïve people can accept the self-sacrificial nature of the covenant with Jesus and apply it to themselves. Yet there are plenty of bad people who are willing to impose this covenant on others to rule them.

It is interesting to note that Christianity conquered the Western world through the powerful example of the self-sacrifice of good-hearted people, namely, the martyrs.

Thousands and thousands of people, over more than three centuries, were willing to be sacrificed for the God of Israel. The slaughter only ceased when Christianity finally conquered the man whose power it needed, the Roman Emperor. Until this was accomplished, Christian martyrs lived a terrible life to satisfy their god's thirst for blood.

In 306 CE, Constantine became both the Roman emperor and a Christian. In 313 CE, he issued the Edict of Milan, ending the Christian persecution. In 380 CE, Theodosius issued the Edict of Thessalonica, making Christianity the official religion of the Roman Empire. Thereafter, the practice of polytheism was gradually extinguished in all Roman lands; eventually, polytheists were persecuted and killed throughout the Empire, including Egypt.

The Roman Emperor chose to impose the Christian faith by shedding Roman blood in Roman territory, and in doing so, he was fulfilling the Abrahamic Law: making sure that only the God of Israel was venerated and spreading the Abrahamic sacred texts throughout the world as Jesus had commanded.

Thus, in addition to sacrificing people in war, the Roman Emperor began to sacrifice his own people as those who clung to the old tradition came to be seen as dissidents from the new faith. This was done to satisfy the desires of the Abrahamic demon of intolerance, hatred, and genocide, as we can now recognize.

Under polytheism, people could live in peace out of political affairs. But when the monotheistic Abrahamic *god* arrived, peace was no longer possible. The envious Abrahamic demon was well on his way toward achieving his second goal, which was to win his war against the other gods by eliminating their veneration from all parts of the world and build his own Empire.

Islam: The Abrahamic Dictatorship

While Christianity was doing its job of eradicating polytheism in Roman territory, the largest and most powerful empire in the world at that time, the Abrahamic demon was sowing another even bloodier religion in the Arabic peninsula: Islam.

If Judaism and Christianity had been strict religions, Islam rose above them both. Islamic law is still more severe, and the punishment of dissidents is terrible. Islam can in fact be seen as the dictatorship of the Abrahamic demon.

The rise of Islam followed the typical pattern in the Abrahamic tradition, by which a prophet emerges who claims to have seen the God of Israel proclaiming that people are not living and worshiping the right way and that they are deviating from their god.

In the case of Islam, this prophet was Muhammad, who was born in the year 570 in Mecca.

In his forties, he claimed to have received a visit from the angel Gabriel, and then he began to preach publicly that:

- God was one.
- People needed to be completely submissive to God.
- He was the prophet and messenger of God.

In short, he delivered almost the same message as the other Abrahamic prophets.

At that time, people in the Arabic peninsula were polytheists living in peace outside political affairs, which was the typical state of life in polytheistic environments. In Mecca, for example, the Kaaba shrine housed 360 idols belonging to various tribes, who worshiped their different gods side by side without conflict.

However, in the sixth century, Judaism and Christianity began to spread into the region, which disturbed the political peace of the area, as monotheistic religions usually do. Under monotheism, there is no space for alternative beliefs and practices.

Thus, at the time of Muhammad's rise, the intolerance of monotheism toward polytheism had already begun to produce instability in the region. Initially, Muhammad received a poor reception from the polytheistic people; for now, there would be three monotheistic religions causing trouble instead of two.

Muhammad then began to impose his religious dictatorship over the world through violence, offering each person the choice between Islam and death.

As you can imagine, the Jews and Christians saw Muhammad as a false prophet. The consequence, of course, was war or, in other words, human sacrifice for their god, the Abrahamic demon.

In the end, the Muslims conquered the Middle East so thoroughly that by 639 CE, they were campaigning to conquer Egypt, which they accomplished in 646 CE.

Over the next few centuries, by executing millions in true human sacrifices for their god, the Abrahamic demon, the followers of Islam conquered many countries in the Middle East, Europe, Africa, and Asia!

The Theological Perspective of Truth and Reality

As everything was created by the creator-God, truth and reality are divine manifestations as well.

Consequently, from the same philosophy we have used to answer the other theological questions, we can say that if truth and reality are accessible to one person to fathom, scrutinize, and appreciate them, they are also available to all the other people.

As you philosophize over some matter, you either obtain the answer for that question or do not get the answer. Moreover, every time someone understands some truth and an aspect of reality, this person needs to be able to explain it to the others.

Accordingly, either you have faith, or you understand something by philosophizing over it. However, faith is individual, whereas philosophy is universal and accessible to anyone.

This is why the down-to-Earth ancient Egyptians built all their civilization over philosophy, not over faith.

Differing from any Abrahamic religion that is built over and by faith in some kind of prophesied revelation by some transcendental being who had appeared to some person, the ancient Egyptian religion was philosophized; in this way, it was reliable as a base for a civilization.

It can be difficult to understand truth and reality, but they are divinely expressed in everything present in the existing universe.

Concluding this theological investigation, if someone tells you that only they can understand truth or reality and that everyone needs to have faith in him or her without any question or explanation, we can be certain that we are facing either a naive, unwise, and over-confident person or a charlatan.

Book III

The Monotheistic Era

The Era of Oppression

Torture

Genocide

Polytheism Vanished

In 476 CE, less than 100 years after monotheism was imposed on the Romans and Egyptians through Christianity, these two great polytheistic civilizations had fallen, and the Middle Ages had begun.

Less than 100 years of Abrahamic monotheism was sufficient to destroy these two prosperous civilizations that had lasted for thousands of years: the Roman civilization had lasted for more than 1,000 years and the Egyptian for approximately 5,600 years. Today, due to the tremendous influence of the Abrahamic monotheistic religions, a few countries are polytheistic.

The Abrahamic Demon's Objective

Now that our civilization has spent two millennia under the domination of the Abrahamic religions, we can undoubtedly see the consequences of following these blind faiths. From these consequences, it is possible to determine, without doubt, that the Abrahamic demon's goals were as follows:

- To sow Intolerance and Hatred that would cause genocide or human sacrifice
- To eliminate human reverence for worship of and devotion to the genuine gods

In these chapters, we will look in depth at the developments within the Abrahamic religions and show how, devastatingly although unsurprisingly, monotheism has given birth to atheism and the materialistic theories.

It can be hard for modern people to grasp that in the polytheistic era, people understood and lived with the fact that there were many gods, even if a particular person chose to worship only one of these; conversely, in our modern monotheistic era, people believe that there really is only one god. Ironically, if someone worships another god, Abrahamic monotheists assume that that person is worshiping a demon and practicing witchcraft, and hence needs to be eliminated.

This is why there have been and still are religious wars in the Abrahamic world. Religious wars have been a part of the Abrahamic domain since its beginning.

Because the Abrahamic god's teachings are self-contradictory and confusing, people must make their own choices regarding how to worship and obey him. Each church worships God in its own way, but if someone worships in a different way, the disagreeing parties look at each other with suspicion, thinking that the other is worshiping a demon and that these dissenting devotees need to be killed in the name of the God of Israel as he commanded the Abrahamic prophets to teach.

Throughout the centuries, the God of Israel has repeatedly got what he wants: human bloodshed.

The monotheistic era is the era of Intolerance, Hatred, and Genocides.

The Scientific Revolution: Separating Science and Religion

It is important to observe that under polytheism, not only was there no separation between religion and science but also everything fell under the purview of religion in the sense that everything in reality was seen as a manifestation of a divine power.

How, then, was religion and science separated?

It was a simple consequence of the fact that under Abrahamic monotheism, everything needs to be explained through the teachings of the prophets of the God of Israel, yet at the same time, the God of Israel is not believed to be involved in any natural phenomena, more than that, this god is believed to overcome natural phenomena through "miracles." If that god was related to certain particular natural phenomena, as it was the case in polytheism, this would seem to his followers to limit his power over the entire creation, as his power would then be tied to one particular aspect of creation.

How could science develop in the context of this monotheistic religion, given that the God of Israel and the prophets were occupied primarily with political problems? As we read in the Bible, their main concern was conquering lands and wealth, and subjugating people to their god's command while eliminating people seen as enemies.

Jesus's famous Sermon on the Mount provides a prime example of the intolerance of the Abrahamic religions.

> "I am the way, and the truth, and the life. No one comes to the Father except through me. If you had known me, you would have known my Father also. From now on, you do know him and have seen him."

And in Matthew 28 we read:

> "Then Jesus came to them and said, '**All authority** in heaven and **on earth** has been given to me. Therefore, go and make disciples of all nations, baptizing them in the name of the Father and of the Son and of the Holy Spirit, and teaching them to **obey everything** I have commanded you. And surely I am with you always, to the very end of the age.'"

In the Abrahamic religions, there is no room for scientific discovery, and there is no tolerance for philosophical discussions of the nature of the cosmos unless these discussions adhere strictly to Biblical teachings. Remember that the jealous God of Israel hates all other gods and everything that comes from them; thus, because the study of science and all natural phenomena might open people's eyes to the manifestations of other gods, scientific research was prohibited as well.

The only way to develop knowledge was to separate science from religion; this finally occurred during the Scientific Revolution. This separation was done in the seventeenth century, more than a millennium after when Jesus was alive. It took this long for Western civilization to free its philosophy from the confines of a barbarian religion.

By the 1600s, polytheism had been dead for more than a millennium, such that no one remembered its existence in detail. In the resulting monotheistic world, a scientist or philosopher would not be accused of worshiping another god; rather, they would be charged of practicing witchcraft if their findings contradicted the official view of the church.

So how could scientists avoid being accused of witchcraft? The solution was simple: they posited that when they were studying science, they were dealing only with earthly elements, and never with transcendental factors. The only way out was to divide reality into two parts, the earthly elements and transcendental elements. The physical world belonged to science, and the transcendental world belonged to religion.

The "genius" who proposed this was René Descartes. If he had suggested returning to polytheism, he would undoubtedly have been burned at the stake to satisfy the God of Israel.

This was not the case under Egyptian polytheism, where everything could be studied freely, with the intention of discovering unknown divine powers and developing those already known for human avail, to approximate humans to the very gods: the ancient Egyptian priests were the philosophers and scientists of ancient times.

Science and religion can develop together, as one thing, under a polytheistic religion; in this case, there is no necessity of separating the two aspects of the universe, because every phenomenon in nature or society reflects a kind of divine power made available to us by a god.

The role of scientists in Western society since the Scientific Revolution can be compared to that of the ancient Egyptian priests. Our scientists can almost be considered the new "priests" in our society. The difference between today and ancient times is that modern scientists are always trying to deny that their work has anything to do with the transcendental world.

It is necessary that you understand the extreme lengths to which this modern divorce has gone.

This division requires that religion be prohibited from dealing with earthly elements such as nature and that science be prohibited from dealing with transcendental elements. Hence, even if scientists today do not need to fear the possibility of being burned at the stake by the church for using science to study both material and transcendental subjects, they still fear that other scientists destroy their reputations and careers by labeling them frauds for not confining their inquiries to the physical realm.

Do you understand the damage that Abrahamic monotheism has caused through the centuries?

In a strict monotheistic culture, if someone wants to be in contact with the metaphysical aspect of life, he or she needs to go to the one "true" church. No transcendence outside that Abrahamic church is considered good; if something else provides a spiritual experience, it is considered demon's worship or witchcraft.

The Abrahamic Religious Wars: Requiring the Greatest Human Sacrifices

The clashes between the Abrahamic religions and others and those between the three branches of Abrahamic religion have already caused the deaths of millions of people.

We have the Jewish genocide of the 20th century, the Christian persecution of polytheists from ancient times up through the 19th century, the early modern religious wars among the Christians, the wars between Christians and Muslims, and the Muslims' persecution of any other religion

The same pattern always occurs: an Abrahamic religion claims that everyone needs to worship its god according to a set of strict rules, then accuses other religions of having false prophets or claim that their way of worship is wrong. Therefore, the Abrahamic religious texts and followers, all other religions are worshiping a devil, not the true god.

Unsurprisingly, Islam is not different. After Muhammad died, Islam broke into two sects: the Sunni and the Shiites, who were always fighting each other. Have they ever achieved peace since then? No. Today we can see the Islamic State (ISIS) with its many followers and many other branches of Islam rising throughout the world, fighting to establish what they call "true Islam" while shedding human blood to satisfy the demon they called God.

Throughout all history, no religions have caused more human sacrifices and violent deaths than everyone of the Abrahamic religions: Judaism, Christianity, and Islam.

It is shocking how people can somehow overlook the fact that the Abrahamic religions require human sacrifice! If human sacrifice is not demanded directly by these religions, it is made in the name of some offspring of Abrahamic monotheism in the culture, as we will see later.

Separating State and Religion

In the Egyptian polytheistic religion and culture, the power of the state authorities was seen as a reflection of divine power, and this power was required to be used to pursue equilibrium in society.

In a monotheistic society, specifically in an Abrahamic society, wherein religion is tangled up with the state, the power of the state authorities is seen as a divine power, but, in contrast to ancient Egyptian government, this power is required to be used to force that monotheism on everyone.

What a difference.

Let's remember what René Descartes started in the 17th century. To study science, he proposed that all physical phenomena were devoid of spirit and machine-like. Stripped of all possibility of transcendental engagement, science was then called *rational thought*; as such, it began to replace religion as the ultimate authority.

In their constant search for more power, the kings of Descartes' time tried to use this new worldview to move away religion from the state. Now the kingship, once regarded as the earthly manifestation of divine power, was divided between two rulers: the king, who ruled absolutely, and the pope.

During this era, religion and the state were still one, but with an interesting difference: the king took care of the daily affairs of life on Earth, and the pope took care of spiritual concerns: the king went to war, the pope went to the church to pray.

Welcome to the absolutism that seized Europe in the 1600s, the political consequence of the Scientific Revolution.

But there is a problem here. The Scientific Revolution had split everything into physical and spiritual elements, convincing people that if something is earthly it can have no transcendental part, and that if something is transcendental it can have no earthly element. Accordingly, the next task was to ascertain what was purely earthly and what was purely metaphysical.

Nevertheless, a transcendental element remained in the state, because the authority of the king was deemed to be an earthly manifestation of a divine power. Thus, government was the one thing that had both earthly and transcendental elements. Yet the state was tasked with focusing only on the physical requirements of life. A state like this was not acceptable to the intellectuals of the time.

Who concerned themselves with every earthly aspect of life after the Scientific Revolution? The scholars. From their perspective, the church needed to concern itself only with the pure metaphysics of life, while the state, because it was responsible for the physical aspects of life, needed to be controlled by those who could take care of the physical elements of life. In this way, the intellectual *Age of Enlightenment* in Europe culminated in the French Revolution of 1789 and other revolutions that completely divorced religion from state affairs.

Because kingship was so strongly associated with divine powers, the monarchy as a whole had to be abolished to enable a complete separation of church and state. The monarchy was replaced with a government made up of strictly physical elements: The Republic.

Abrahamic Monotheism: The Origins of Atheism and Materialism

In the polytheistic era, anyone who did not identify oneself with the worship of a certain god could choose another god to follow. In the monotheistic era, in contrast, anyone who did not identify oneself with the acceptable god was left with no choice but to abandon religion for atheism.

After the Scientific Revolution, when religion had been relegated to its own niche and was no longer consider to mix with the rest of life, it became possible for a person to live without religion, without accepting the existence of anything transcendental. We have no records of atheism in ancient Egypt, but in modern times it is normal and fairly common.

Welcome to Materialism: Everything is matter, nothing is more than matter, only matter matters.

Materialistic Theories: The Daughters of Abrahamic Religion

The promise of materialism is essentially the same as of Abrahamic religion: both systems promise salvation from hell. The difference is that the Abrahamic religion oaths to save people from a literal hell in the afterlife, whereas the materialism vows to save people from hell on Earth.

For materialists, the universe is a mere unconscious soulless object. This includes the food chain, the laws of physics, the existence of death, the reality of pain and suffering in our lives, the necessity to work and produce what we need to survive. Everything in the universe is a problem to be overcome through human intelligence. In fact, materialists believe that human intelligence is the only thing that came out right in this soulless universe, although they believe it came about entirely by accident!

For them, we humans therefore have the obligation to use our astonishing intelligence to overcome the sad inadequacies of the universe. If materialists saw the universe as a living being, they would probably even presume to train it like a dog, so that it would create things as humans saw fit better!

To materialists, if hell exists, it is here on Earth, created by the savage universe. People have only this life, and there is nothing more than that. The transcendental element of religion is therefore absent from materialism although the Abrahamic promise of pursuing paradise and escaping from hell is not.

How do materialists attempt to save people from hell on Earth? How do they try to build their paradise here? There are many theories about how best to achieve that goal. Let's review one that can serve as a key to understanding all the others: communism.

Communism and other similar theories have the same goal as the Abrahamic religions and the same way of achieving it: communists aim to take men to paradise through obedience to commandments and to exterminate anyone who refuses to accept their ways.

The major characteristics of the Abrahamic religions are:

- Monotheistic religion
- The goal of achieving paradise
- The existence of an unbreakable bloody covenant between people and a god
- The requirement to eliminate everyone who worships other gods or disagrees with their god's commandments
- The requirement of strict obedience to the rules without questioning them

Some will argue that communism diverges from this pattern in that it does not include a god. In every Abrahamic religion, there is a prophet who receives commandments from god. In every materialistic theory such as communism, there is an intellectual who *devises* the path to create a paradise on Earth, whereas in religion, the gods are outside a person, in materialistic "religions" such as materialism and communism the gods are inside a person: the god is the brain, and his godly attribute is intelligence. The Abrahamic religions have a transcendental god, but the materialistic theories have an earthly "god," the wonders of the brain. Recall that, for materialists, human intelligence is the sole good thing created in this utterly material universe.

Religious prophets receive visions from their god about salvation from hell. They are the chosen ones. Materialistic intellectuals, meanwhile, have visions wherein they create a theory about how to save humanity from hell on Earth. These founding intellectuals are thereby "chosen" by nature and uniquely endowed with enough intelligence to conceive of a new political order. They think they have *The Brain*.

Communism and other materialistic theories even have the requirement, similar to that seen in the Abrahamic religions, of an unbreakable covenant: to put any such theory into practice, everyone in the entire nation needs to agree with it, and no one can operate outside of it. Anyone who dares to disagree with the new theory needs to be eliminated, including people who worship gods as these gods distract from their allegiance to the theory.

If materialistic theories are not religions, in the sense of the Abrahamic faiths, why then do they prohibit alternate religious practices and demand monotheistic allegiance to the theories above all else?

The rules of these theories need to be followed as strictly as the rule of Abrahamic religions as well. There are so many similarities between Abrahamic religions and materialistic theories that they can be classified as belonging to the same kind of thought system. The unique difference is that the materialistic theories do not embrace transcendental thinking among their postulates.

Most if not all materialistic theories share the same tradition as the Abrahamic religions.

Take a look at some of them:

- Communism
- Socialism
- Nazism (National Socialism)
- Fascism

These four theories have their roots in the same intellectual, Karl Marx. Followers of each of these theories claim that they are following the right way and all others are not. The same dynamic occurs in both Abrahamic religions and materialistic theories: both originate when an "intellectual prophet" claims to have all the answers it needs to transform the world into a paradise.

Then, every time one of these theories is put into practice, nations following different ways fight among themselves.

Hitler, the ruler of Nazi Germany, fought against Stalin, the ruler of the Communist Soviet Union. Mao-Tze Tung, the ruler of Communist China, competed against Leonid Brezhnev, a later ruler of the Communist Soviet Union. Stalin ordered Trotsky and thousands of other people to be killed in his fight for control of the Soviet Union. These are just some examples showing that, in countries where the Abrahamic religions do not reign supreme, their offspring, i.e., the materialistic theories such as communism, socialism, Nazism, and fascism, are nevertheless hard at work sacrificing humans on behalf of their theories.

Jesus predicted this in the Sermon on the Mount:

"Do not think that I have come to abolish the Law or the Prophets; I have not come to abolish them but to fulfill them. For truly, I say to you, until heaven and earth pass away, not an iota, not a dot, will pass from the Law until all is accomplished."

The tradition of the materialistic theories is the same as those of the Abrahamic religions, and the results are identical as well: intolerance and hatred that leads to genocide.

These four theories, when put into practice, have been responsible for more than 100 million people sacrificed, including both wartime and "peace" time, as the rulers often killed those among their own people who disobeyed their commandments. The terrifying thing is that human sacrifice has been performed on this scale in only one century, the twentieth.

Can you see now what were the Abrahamic demon's goals?

- To sow Intolerance and Hatred that leads to genocide or human sacrifice
- To eliminate human reverence for worship of and devotion to the genuine gods

Can you see how the demon has achieved this as well?

How could the materialistic theories have arisen in any cultural environment other than a thoroughly Abrahamic one?

The Inevitable Polytheism: The Natural Rise of the Gods

Despite his attempts, however, we can see polytheism reemerging everywhere.

This is because, even now, no one is worshiping or serving only one being or power. Without realizing it, most people, even self-proclaimed monotheists and atheists, are worshiping many ideals and values as if they were gods. Today most people are worshiping the political state, technology, science, brands, sports teams, music groups, and many other things, showering them with attention, money, and loyalty as if they were gods.

In the Catholic Church, for example, a form of "polytheism" can be seen in the practice of addressing prayers to more than ten thousand saints. Worshippers pray to various saints depending on the saints' specific divine powers or patronages. Doesn't this look extremely similar to ancient Egyptian polytheism, wherein worshippers prayed to whichever god was most closely associated with their particular need?

It is worth noting that the worship of the saints was one of the main reasons why the Protestants broke with the Catholic Church. Worship of any other entities, even the holiest Christians, is actually prohibited by the prophets in the Bible, yet it constantly creeps back in.

To maintain monotheism, it is necessary to continuously suppress the natural polytheism of humanity. Monotheism like the Abrahamic one is always imposed on free people rather than being freely accepted.

Polytheism seems to be natural and inevitable.

The Nation-States: A New Religion or a New God?

When we look at how modern people bond with famous actors, singers, brands, sport teams, and nations or states, among other things, our responses to these public figures and identities are comparable to the responses that people make to their gods in their religions.

The most developed system of worship of an earthly entity has been loyalty to the state. Let's examine the religious elements of this system.

National anthems, to say the less, resemble prayers to a divine state; imposing government buildings looks like temples and are sometimes regarded as just as sacred as the ancient Egyptian temples. Remember, only the high priests could enter the inner-most chambers of the ancient Egyptian temples; in the same way, most government buildings spaces deny access to the common people so that only high-status personnel can enter there to share their knowledge, to get access to their tools, and to discuss secret government operations. Religion is also present in our elections as we typically try to elect the purest candidate who is most devoted to the state as our leader.

The ancient Egyptians would never have been mistaken or confused about the essence of all these objects and entities: all of them would have been openly understood as sacred as the earthly manifestations of transcendental forces and divine power.

Ancient Egypt Emerges Again

You can get an idea of how thoroughly ancient Egyptian culture was suppressed by recalling that by the dawn of European colonialism in Egypt, the entire world had forgotten how to read Egyptian hieroglyphs. Their meaning was finally deciphered in 1822 by a man named Jean-François Champollion.

Now, almost two centuries later, the many unearthed papyri and monumental inscriptions are still being translated into modern languages. Based on what has already been translated, we can begin to comprehend how awe-inspiring the ancient Egyptian civilization, culture, cosmology, philosophy, and religion really were.

At the same time, with every new text translated, it is becoming increasingly obvious that many Abrahamic texts were *inspired* by or even distorted copies from ancient Egyptian literature. Was this accidental plagiarism or intentional fraud? No matter which it was, the scale of this cultural *adoption* is huge, and its effects have lasted for millennia. We are on the brink, in fact, of uncovering the largest fraud in all of human history!

Book IV

Abrahamic Monotheism:
A Literary Investigation

I think most readers are now at least somewhat acquainted with the Abrahamic sacred texts, given their prominent role in Western civilization, even without reading the many quotations from these texts that have already been provided in the present book.

Once we read the ancient Egyptian wisdom poems, then, we cannot help but be reminded of the remarkably similar Biblical texts. The correspondence between the two bodies of literature is undeniable.

Given their similarity, we must ask which came first. Is it more likely that the Abrahamic texts *originated* from the ancient Egyptian ones? Or, on the contrary, did the ancient Egyptians *copy* from the Abrahamic texts?

If the answer is that the Abrahamic prophets copied from the ancient Egyptian wisdom texts, passing stolen knowledge off as their own and using it to conquer the Western world, we are about to reveal the most significant act of plagiarism or fraud in human history.

But regardless of who copied whom, why didn't anyone notice the theft? There were several reasons why, in ancient times, it would have gone unnoticed.

First of all, in ancient times not even 2% of the population had the ability to read and write; in ancient Egypt, not even all of the elites but rather only the scribes were trained to read and write. Furthermore, and most importantly, outside the literate elite, tales were told and passed through the generations orally; in this fashion, many details of the stories such as specific names, places, and authorship were forgotten and changed over time. Furthermore, even people who could read and write did not have access to as much written material as we have now because prior to the invention of printing, everything needed to be copied by hand, which made written literature expensive and scarce.

Second, after ancient Egyptian civilization to be suppressed and buried under the sands of time, no one was able to read and understand Egyptian hieroglyphs. It was not until 1822 that Jean-François Champollion discovered how to understand hieroglyphs. Even after that, it would take more than a century for scholars to translate the surviving writings to recover a sense of ancient Egyptian philosophy from the texts. In this way, it was not until the 20th century that scholars were able to notice the "resemblance" between the texts. By this time, of course, monotheism was already hegemonic on all of Western civilization, and Christian missionaries and Muslims were actively pushing their faith on colonized people all over the world.

Hebrew and Egyptian Languages: Which Came First?

Hebrew belongs to the Canaanite group of languages and came to exist as a spoken language between 1200 and 586 BCE in the Kingdoms of Israel and Judah. Another language common at that time and place was Old Aramaic.

The oldest written inscriptions in either of these languages date from the 10th century BCE.

With the ancient Egyptian language, the case was hugely different. A complete written sentence in ancient Egyptian has been discovered in a tomb in Egypt dating from as early as 2690 BCE, showing that by that time, ancient Egyptian was already a highly developed language. Along with Sumerian, ancient Egyptian is one of the oldest recorded languages in the world.

The texts we will examine here were composed between 2350 and 1640 BCE. Strictly from written evidence, therefore, it appears unlikely that the older ancient Egyptian texts were derived from the younger Abrahamic ones.

Ancient Egyptian Literature

The ancient Egyptian writings can be divided into four categories:

- Theological Texts or Sacred Texts
- Official Inscriptions
- Literary Texts
- Everyday Texts

The Sacred Texts deal with ancient Egyptian mythology, theology, philosophy, cosmogony, and cosmology, as well as all their sacred and *secret* rituals and prayers.

These texts have principally been recovered from the walls of the temples' innermost chambers, from walls inside tombs, and in the papyrus that is known today as "The Egyptian Book of the Dead."

The language used in these texts was broad, highly symbolic but historically accurate, and although it evolved over millennia, this *sacred language* did not change in the way that popular and spoken languages do over time; for this reason, as the centuries went on, only high priests with special training could read and write the sacred language properly (the hieroglyphs).

The sacred texts' protagonists are the gods. Thus, the writers used dramatic and fanciful language to describe the powerful gods' actions and forces but were careful to describe them accurately. The *exception* to this are "The Books of the Dead" (known as pyramid texts), which also features deceased people as characters, but which is nevertheless concerned with transcendental things as the dead were believed to be in the gods' realm in the afterlife. Thus, in general, these texts do not deal with real facts about life on Earth, as this was not their purpose.

It is important to recall that the ancient Egyptians regarded their supremacy at that time as being due to their highly developed knowledge, including their language. Accordingly, they attempted to keep their knowledge safe by restricting it to the elite within their society. This point will be especially important later in our investigation.

Official Inscriptions used the same language as the sacred texts, but they dealt only with the historical facts of ancient Egypt and were mostly related to political events.

These texts were very accurate, although their depictions of the king were idealized; in general, they were not fanciful.

Literary Texts were popular texts, which were recited in public; for this reason, they used more popular words from the spoken form of the language.

In their written form, these texts were used to teach new scribes how to read and write. They can be classified into three styles: Tales, Discourses, and Teachings.

These entertainment-oriented texts talk about real people in ancient Egyptian history, yet they are fanciful and fictional poems, depicting both gods and men as contributing to events on Earth, telling of men's deeds in imaginative and fantastic ways to make them more entertaining for readers and listeners. The purpose was really to enchant people to imprint the wisdom content in their minds, even we can think that they were used as political propaganda for foreigners to awe them.

There are two important features of these texts that we must keep in mind for our investigation.

First, they never disclose the details of sacred rituals: even when they mention rituals performed for the gods, they simplify and distorted their descriptions to such an extent that it would not be possible for a reader to reenact the true ritual based on the text alone.

Second, although they present a great deal of content that seems to be obscure to readers who are not ancient Egyptians, these *obscure* elements were never a symbolic way of teaching their religious secrets; rather, this was the traditional ancient Egyptian way of talking about their daily life, environment, and happenings.

These texts talk about people, usually kings and their descendants, who were already dead at the time of the texts' creation;

accordingly, they always refer to these kings as gods as the kings were considered to be gods in the afterlife. It is crucial, however, to note one feature of the ancient Egyptian religion: although they would not talk this way about a living king, when they talk about a deceased king, they refer to him as divine even when referring to his life on Earth and even when referring to him as an infant or an embryo! This characteristic is the key element to understand how the Israelites incorrectly interpreted the ancient Egyptian literary texts that they *appropriated* to create their Abrahamic texts.

The Thesis

The purpose of this section is to show the many similarities between ancient Egyptian and Abrahamic texts and to prove that these similarities could have arisen by accident or must have been the result of an intentional *appropriation* of ideas.

The first similarity we can clearly identity is the style of the literature. Both the ancient Egyptian literary texts and the Abrahamic ones use fanciful language, both depict men and gods jointly affecting outcomes on earth, and both depict earthly historical events in spectacular language that makes the stories more entertaining.

Keeping in mind that most people were not literate and therefore transmitted their wisdom literature orally, it was easy for people who were not acquainted with ancient Egyptian traditions to misunderstand the tradition of depicting deceased kings as gods. This is how the Israelites came to believe, mistakenly, that the ancient Egyptian literary texts were talking about gods' words and deeds rather than the kings'.

The ancient Egyptian wisdom texts refer sometimes to specific gods but sometimes simply to "God." When ancient Egyptians used the word "God," they could have been referring to a particular god from the author's temple or city or they could have been referring to the king, either a particular king or sometimes the kingship itself, because the king was regarded as the god Atum's deputy on earth, responsible for maintaining order here. Pay attention to how the ancient Egyptian literary texts depict kings' deeds as if they were a god's deeds. For someone not acquainted with ancient Egyptian traditions, this would be extremely confusing.

Another change that the Israelites apparently made in their translations was to rename the Egyptian gods after their features or their animal appearance; for example, the god Bastet became a cat or a lion in the Abrahamic scriptures, and Atum became the creator-God, the creator of all things, or the self-created one. Such "misinterpretations" could have happened easily given that the ancient Egyptian texts were written in the Egyptian language and the followers of the God of Israel had to translate them into an

Israelite language, which was a Canaanite language, that was only a spoken language with poor vocabulary for many centuries.

In the bibliography chapter you can check various books to read many ancient Egyptian tales in their entirety.

I will begin by quoting some of their literary texts and lastly, I will use a pyramid text; all of them with some commentaries between the verses and parenthetical comments on possible variant translations of certain gods' names.

Summing up the thesis it can be told that the Jewish bible, or the Old Testament was sourced from ancient Egyptian literary texts, yet the Christian texts, the New Testament was sourced either from those texts but also from some of those ancient Egyptian sacred ones as we will read later.

The Loyalist's Teaching

This teaching is written in the voice of a priest who teaches loyalty to the king.

> *"Beginning of the Teaching made by the leader of nobility, chief of action made by a man for his son father of the god, beloved of the god, master of secrets of the house of the king, may he live, flourish and be well, overlord of the land to its limit sem-priest, controller of the kilted man as a teaching before his children,*
>
> *'Let me say what is great, may you listen, as I cause you to know the manner of eternity, a matter of live in truth, of proceeding to revered status.'*

In the verse above, "father of the god" is a title for a class of priests; naming a priest "father of the god" probably was a way to convey to the role of that priest an Egyptian idea that a father was a provider and guarantor of means, caress, protection, and prosperity for his offspring. Yet below, we can read them calling the kings the god Ra, the gods' chief once the Pharaohs were manifesting the power of the god Ra on earth through the kingship.

> *"'Praise the king within your bodies!*
>
> *Embrace His Majesty in your hearts.*
>
> *Spread awe of him every day.*
>
> *Create acclamation for him at every moment.*
>
> *He is the Insight into what is in hearts, his eyes probe everybody.*
>
> *He is the sungod [Ra] in whose leadership people live.*
>
> *Whoever is under his light will be great in wealth.*
>
> *He is the sungod by whose rays people see.*
>
> *He is the one who brightens the Two Lands, more than the sun.'"*

The Two Lands here are Upper and Lower Egypt. The Nile flows from Upper Egypt in the southern uplands to Lower Egypt in the northern delta region. Not knowing where the source of the Nile was, the ancient Egyptians imagined that the Nile's waters came from the sky goddess Nut in the gods' domain, which must therefore somehow connect to Upper Egypt. In other texts we will read references to the "King of the Two Lands." It is possible that outsiders mistranslated this as "the King of Earth and Heave.n.

> *"'His heat scorches more than the flame of a torch, He is more devouring in his moment than fire.*
>
> *He is more fertile than the great Flood of the Nile, he has filled the Two Lands* [Earth and Heaven] *with the trees of life.*
>
> *Noses are blocked when he falls to raging.*
>
> *When he is peaceful, people breathe his air.*
>
> *He grants sustenance for anyone who follows him,*
>
> *and feeds the one who keeps his paths.*
>
> *The man he favors will be a lord of wealth, the one he rejects will be a nobody.*
>
> *The servant of the king will be blessed,*
>
> *[...] his opponents casted away.*
>
> *It is his power that fights for him - slaughter is what spreads respect for him.*
>
> *Watching over [...]*
>
> *Your [...] is founded upon the praise of his beauty.*
>
> *He opens up the creation [...]*
>
> *[...] that his heart desires, He is life to the man who gives him adoration.*
>
> *His opponents will be beneath distress. Their corpses are thrown into the water.*
>
> *Sustenance is the king; Abundance is his speech.*
>
> *He is one who creates in his essence.*
>
> *He is the heir of every god, the champion of the one who created him.*
>
> *They strike down his opponents for him.*
>
> *See His Majesty may he live, flourish and be well, is in his palace of life, prosperity, health.*

He is Atum [creator-God or creator, simply] of joining necks.

His protection is behind the man who promotes his power.

He is Khnum [craftsman] for everybody, the begetter who brings the people into being.

He is Bastet [Lion or Lioness], she who protects the Two Lands, he is praised for his sheltering.

He is Sekhmet [the plagues] against the one who transgresses what he has commanded.

The one whom he disfavors will be in distress.

Fight for his name; purify in his life.

Avoid the instant of laziness.

The servant of the king will have rewarded, but there can be no tomb for one who rebels against His Majesty - his corpse will be something cast into the water.

Do not restrain from the presents of his giving.

Pay homage to the Bee, adore his White Crown, worship the one who raises the Double Crown.

As you do this, your bodies will be well, you can find it to be so for eternity.'

The Egyptian king was told "the king of Double Crown," i.e., the kind of Upper Land (White Crown) and the Lower Land (Red Crown). By foreigners, this phrase could have been mistakenly translated as the Kingdom of Earth and Heaven.

"'Enter the land by the gift of the king.

Rest in the place of eternity!

United with the cavern of the one within everlasting time, with the shrine of your children bearing your love, and your heirs remaining in your positions.

Copy my example, do not neglect my words!

Put into effect the rule I have drawn up.

Speak then to your children for the word has taught since the time of Ra.

I am a noble to be heard, whose lord has entered his reflections.

Do not pass by my example, do not be indifferent from my talent.

The son who hears will be without any evils.

Does not every plan succeed by it?

You will be praising this after years - faithfulness to them assures success.

Another method to guide your hearts, as something to good effect before your workers:

be careful with people, organize your staff together, and fasten on the Majesty of those who do.

It is people who bring what exists into being.

We live as men who have by their hands.

If there is a lack of it, poverty prevails.

It is professions that produce offerings.

The one whose house is empty, his foundation shivers - their voices strengthen the walls.

The man who sleeps till dawn is the lord of a people; there can be no sleep for the solitary man.

A lion is not sent on a mission.

There is no herd that can be tied to the wall; its voice is like someone thirsty behind a well,

with decay around it, more than fattened birds.

People desire the flood of Nile, and they find it, but there is no plowed field that creates itself.

The herd is large when the herdsman; it is the fettered bull that drive the dueller.

It is the herdsman who brings the animal to land.

Will be a man of many flocks without number, the professions [...] of the god.

Anyone who is experienced in it, is a clever man.

Do not overwhelm the field-labourer with taxes.

A man who complains, does he return to you next year?

If he is alive, you have his arms, but if you ruin him, his thoughts turn him to laziness.

Fix the tax-levy according to the grain harvested.

A just man is the one who is in the heart of the god.

There can be no opportunity for possessions for an evil man; his children do not find his properties for inheritance.

The hard man causes the end of his life; his children will not be his devotees.

Serfs will be for the one who passes him; there can be no heir for the mean-spirited.

A lord of followers is great in respect.

The strident man is an evil on the heart.

It is the evil man who destroys his home ground, and the loved man for whom a city is founded.

Patience is the monument of a man.

Silence is good for [...].

The man who foresee what must come has never been frustrated.

The man with power in a task prevails.

Does the cow reproduce for the hard man?

A herdsman of evil brings misery to his herd.

Fight for people in every respect.

*They are the flock that is good for their **lord**.*

It is they who find what one lives on, so they are good too for burial.

See ... [...]

Watch over your funerary-priests; if the son is lazy, there is still the pure-priest.

The one called an heir is the one who does favor.

Initiate the noble and invocate in his name.

Honor the blessed dead, bring the food-offerings!

For doing is more useful to the doer than to the one for whom it is done.

It is the nourished dead who protect the one who is on earth.'

So, it ends, from start to finish, as found in writing."

The last phrase is a common concluding phrase in ancient literary texts alerting the apprentice scribes who copied these texts that the text had indeed come to an end.

In this poem we can clearly see many similarities to the Abrahamic wisdom texts, especially since we know that Abrahamic readers would have interpreted all references to kings as references to God, not as a deceased king. The style, expressions, commandments, and promises of good and bad earthly consequences for good and bad choices are strikingly similar.

Because this text is one of the shortest ones, I was able to quote it here in its entirety. The following texts are more lengthy and so will be represented by the most relevant excerpts.

The Tale of Sinuhe

This tale is important for our investigation in that it shows how easily foreign translators may have become *confused* about the word "God." The original text uses the word "God" to refer alternately to the king, the principal god of a city, and the God who is the most important for whom is speaking in the tale.

Further, it opens with an account that is astonishingly and undeniably similar to the accounts of Jesus' resurrection.

This text narrates the adventures of Sinuhe, a royal courtier. After his king dies, he becomes desperate and runs away from Egypt to escape from a possible conspiracy in the court of the new king. He rebuilds his life in a foreign land, raises a family, and becomes famous and rich. But at the end of his life, he is summoned home by Egypt's new king to return to his motherland before he dies.

This tale is written in the voice of the deceased Sinuhe as if he were narrating his life.

> *"The Erpā, the Duke, the Chancellor of the King of the North, the judge, the Āntchmer of the marches, the King in the lands of the Nubians, the veritable royal kinsman loving him, the member of the royal bodyguard, Sinuhe, says: 'I am a member of the bodyguard of his lord, the servant of the King, and of the house of Neferit, the feudal chieftainess, the Erpāt princess, the highly favoured lady, the royal wife of Usertsen, whose word is truth in Khnemetast, the royal daughter of Amenemhāt, whose word is truth in Qanefer.*
>
> *On the seventh day of the third month of the season Akhet, in the thirtieth year [of his reign], the god drew nigh to his horizon, and the King of the South, the King of the North, Sehetepabrā, ascended into heaven, and was invited to the sun, and his divine members mingled with those of him that made him. The King's House was in silence, hearts were bowed down in sorrow, the two Great Gates were shut fast, the officials sat motionless, and the people mourned.'"*

The phrase "The God ascended to his horizon" refers to the king's death. Here, we have a perfect pattern prefiguring Jesus's resurrection, which his first followers apparently understood in a way that was in keeping with ancient Egyptian beliefs about the afterlife. Jesus's resurrection is described in Christian scripture as an ascension to a life together with God, to an existence that combines a sort of divine flesh with human nature. In fact, the Christian texts depict Jesus and God as being "one" in the same manner that ancient Egyptian texts describe their kings as being both human and divine after death! Later in this tale we will see more references to this kind of divine essence of deceased kings.

For comparison, here is a passage about Jesus's resurrection from the book known as 1 Peter in the Bible.

> "It saves you by the resurrection of Jesus Christ, who has gone into heaven and is at God's right hand—with angels, authorities, and powers in submission to him."

Continuing with the tale, in the next passage Sinuhe has already left Egypt and is in his new home discussing his fate with a friendly foreigner.

> "'How I came to be brought into this country I know not; it was, perhaps, by the Providence of God.'
>
> And Āmmuiansha [the foreigner] said unto me, 'What will become of the land without that beneficent god, the terror of whom passed through the lands like the goddess Sekhmet in a year of pestilence?'
>
> Then I made answer unto him, saying, 'His son shall save us. He has entered the Palace and has taken possession of the heritage of his father. Moreover, he is **the god who has no equal, and no other can exist beside him**, the lord of wisdom, perfect in his plans, of good will when he passes decrees, and one comes forth and goes in according to his ordinance."

Note the different meanings of the word "God" in this passage above. In the first phrase Sinuhe uses it to refer to the god whom he worships the most, perhaps the god of his birth city. Shortly after that, he uses the same word god to refer to the deceased Pharaoh. It is important to note that as both of the Pharaohs in this tale (father and son) were dead at that time of the tale's composition, both are referred to as God.

Also note how in the last two lines, this tale speaks of the king with reverence equal to that used by the Abrahamic prophets in talking about their God. In fact, it is reminiscent of the first commandment issued by the Abrahamic God: "you shall have no other gods before me."

Throughout the remainder of this excerpt, Sinuhe will continue to refer to his Pharaoh as the god, against whom no one can fight and win.

> "'He reduced foreign lands to submission whilst his father sat in the Palace directing him in the matters which had to be carried out. He is mighty of valor, he slayed with his sword, and in bravery he has no compeer.
>
> His heart is bold when he sees the battle array, he permits none to sit down behind.
>
> His face is fierce as he rushes on the attacker.
>
> He rejoices when he takes captive the chief of a band of desert robbers.
>
> He seizes his shield, he rains blows upon him, but he has no need to repeat his attack, for he slays his foe before he can hurl his spear at him.
>
> Before he draws his bow the nomads have fled, his arms are like the souls of the Great Goddess.
>
> He fights, and if he reaches his object of attack, he spares not, and he leaves no remnant.
>
> He is beloved, his pleasantness is great, he is the conqueror, and his town loves him more than herself.'"

This content above is similar to that in some Abrahamic texts, depicting God as both capable of enjoying the destruction of a people seen as barbarian and, at the same time, kind, sweet, and lovely as we read in chapters before.

In another verse glorifying the king, Sinuhe speaks of the king as God even when he was in his mother's womb:

> "'He was king and conqueror before his birth, and he has worn his crowns since he was born.

He has multiplied births, and he it is whom God has made to be the joy of this land, which he has ruled, and the boundaries of which he has enlarged.

He has conquered the Lands of the South, shall he not conquer the Lands of the North?'"

Compare this to how Christians wrote about Jesus as being a god even when he was in his mother's womb, for example, in the account recorded in the Bible's Gospel of Matthew:

"This is how the birth of Jesus the Messiah came about: His mother Mary was pledged to be married to Joseph, but before they came together, she was found to be pregnant through the Holy Spirit. Because Joseph her husband was faithful to the law, and yet did not want to expose her to public disgrace, he had in mind to divorce her quietly.

But after he had considered this, an angel of the Lord appeared to him in a dream and said, "Joseph son of David, do not be afraid to take Mary home as your wife, because what is conceived in her is from the Holy Spirit. She will give birth to a son, and you are to give him the name Jesus, because he will save his people from their sins."

All this took place to fulfill what the Lord had said through the prophet: "The virgin will conceive and give birth to a son, and they will call him Immanuel (which means 'God with us')."

After on, we read many stanzas recounting the successful life of Sinuhe. Finally, in his old age, he is summoned by the new Pharaoh to return to Egypt. When facing his new king for the first time, he says to him:

"... I found His Majesty seated upon the Great Throne in the umtet chamber of silver-gold. I arrived there, I raised myself up after my prostrations, and I knew not that I was in his presence.

Then this god [i.e. the King] *spoke unto me harshly, and I became like unto a man who is confounded in the darkness; my intelligence left me, my limbs quaked, my heart was no longer in my body, and I knew not whether I was dead or alive.'"*

111

This stanza above resembles some of the Abrahamic prophets' visions of God. The Jewish prophet Daniel, for example, reports in Chapter 10 of the book bearing his name that "the sound of his words came to my ears, and on hearing his voice I went into a deep sleep with my face to the earth."

Chapter 5 of the Book 2 Chronicles claims that, when the spirit of God entered a temple where people were gathered, "the priests could not stand to minister by reason of the cloud: for the glory of the Lord had filled the house of God."

As for the Christian scriptures, the author of the Book of Revelation states that "when I saw [God], I went down on my face at his feet as one dead."

In the Gospel of John, people even responded this way to the living Jesus just before his arrest: "As soon as he had said unto them, I am he, they went backward, and fell to the ground."

The stylistic exaggeration in the Bible echoes that which we see in ancient Egyptian fiction poems. The descriptions of heaven and God's throne in Abrahamic tales may be exaggerations of the lavishly decorated Egyptian court, which could only be seen by people who had been specially summoned to appear. As the majority of people would never enter the throne room, you can imagine the dramatic descriptions of the appearance of the royal palaces that would have been shared by the select few who had been invited.

It is important to remember that the ancient Egyptians and probably other peoples of the time believed that the sacred works of art in the throne room, including the statues, had life. This may shed light on the descriptions in the Abrahamic texts of fantastical living beings, such as seraphim, in the throne room.

We need to keep in mind that these texts were created to be fantastic and imaginative. Thus, the statues were depicted as not merely sacred but actually living. The bible's seraphim calling to one another *"Holy, holy, holy is the Lord Almighty; the whole earth is full of his glory"* may have been merely a fantastic way of describing the palace sphinxes, for example.

The Tale of the Shipwrecked Traveler

As this tale is not so long, I have quoted it in its entirety.

This tale represents the same kind of fiction that we read in Genesis, wherein, a speaking serpent lives together with humans.

This tale also provides good examples of how ancient Egyptian texts referred elusively to their sacred rituals, describing them in ways that would not allow readers to recreate the real ancient Egyptian rituals; in another great clue that the Abrahamic texts were copied by foreigners, with limited understanding, from ancient Egyptian popular literature, this tale depicts offerings to the gods in the same way as they are depicted in Abrahamic texts.

This tale is about a sailor who is desperate over his failed mission. Another sailor comforts him by sharing his own terrible travel experience and advises him on how to tell the king of his failure.

Note the similarities between this tale and the well-known tale of the Garden of Eden: both feature a paradise that is full of fruit trees, but that is also home to a behemoth serpent who is also a god (remember the chapters where we read that there were many gods in the Garden of Eden) and that land will never be seen again by anyone after the protagonists have departed.

> *"A certain servant of wise understanding have said: 'Let your heart be of good cheer, O Prince!*
>
> *Verily we have arrived at our homes. The mallet has been grasped, and the anchor-post has been driven into the ground, and the bow of the boat has grounded on the bank.*
>
> *Thanksgivings have been offered up to God, and every man has embraced his neighbor. Our sailors have returned in peace and safety, and our fighting men have lost none of their comrades, even though we travelled to the uttermost parts of Wawat (Nubia), and through the country of Senmut (Northern Nubia). Verily we have arrived in peace, and we have reached our own land again.*
>
> *Listen, O prince, unto me, even though I be a poor man. Wash yourself, and let water run over your fingers. I would that you*

should be ready to return an answer to the man who addresses you, and to speak to the King from your heart, and assuredly you must give thine answer promptly and without hesitation.

The mouth of a man delivers him, and his words provide a covering for his face. Act you according to the promptings of your heart, and when you have spoken you will have made him to be at rest.

I will now speak and give you a description of the things that once happened to me myself when I was journeying to the copper mines of the king.

I went down into the sea in a ship that was one hundred and fifty cubits (225 feet) in length, and forty cubits (60 feet) in breadth, and it was manned by one hundred and fifty sailors who were chosen from among the best sailors of Egypt.

They had looked upon the sky, they had looked upon the land, and their hearts were more understanding than the hearts of lions.

Now although they were able to say beforehand when a tempest was coming and could tell when a squall was going to rise before it broke upon them, a storm actually overtook us when we were still on the sea. Before we could make the land, the wind blew with redoubled violence, and it drove before it upon us a wave that was eight cubits (12 feet) high.

A plank was driven towards me by it, and I seized it; and as for the ship, those who were therein perished, and not one of them escaped.

Then a wave of the sea bore me along and cast me up upon an island, and I passed three days there by myself, with none but mine own heart for a companion; I laid me down and slept in a hollow in a thicket, and I hugged the shade. And I lifted up my legs [i.e. walked about]*, so that I might find out what to put in my mouth, and I found there figs and grapes, and all kinds of fine large berries; and there were there gourds, and melons, and pumpkins as large as barrels, and there were also there fish and water-fowl.*

There was no food of any sort or kind that did not grow in this island. And when I had eaten all I could eat, I laid the remain-

*der of the food upon the ground, for it was too much for me to carry in my arms. I then dug a hole in the ground and made a fire, and **I prepared pieces of wood and a burnt-offering for the gods.**'"*

The ancient Egyptians never burned their offerings to the gods. Instead, if they were offering meat, they slaughtered the animals far from the altar, then cooked everything that needed cooking and offered a fully prepared meal, as if for a human, to the gods at the shrine. The last ceremony in each ritual, in fact, was "the reversion of the offerings," when priests would enter the god's chamber to take back the offerings, which the priests would then eat as a communion with the gods. Here is an example of how that ceremony would have looked in a ritual to the god Djehuty (known also as Thoth), the god of words, knowledge, and wisdom.

"O Djehuty, your enemy withdraws for you. Heru has turned himself to his Eye in its name of 'Reversion-of-offerings.' I am Djehuty. I come to perform this rite for Djehuty, might of Heka-power.

These, your divine offerings revert, they revert to your servants for life, for stability, for health, and for joy! O that the Eye of Heru may flourish for you eternally!"

The sailor continues the tale of his experiences on the island.

*"'And I heard a sound as of thunder, which I thought to be caused by a wave of the sea, and the trees rocked and the earth quaked, and I covered my face. And I found that the sound was caused by a **serpent** that was coming towards me. It was thirty cubits (45 feet) in length, and its beard was more than two cubits in length, and its body was covered with scales of gold, and the two ridges over its eyes were of pure lapis-lazuli; and it coiled its whole length up before me. And it opened its mouth to me, now I was lying flat on my stomach in front of it, and it said unto me, 'Who has brought you here? Who hath brought you here, O miserable one? Who has brought you here?*

*If you do not immediately declare unto me who has brought you to this island, I will make you to know what it is to be burnt with fire, and you will **become ashes**, a thing that is invisible.'"*

Here, we have another remarkable similarity to the story from Genesis, where the Abrahamic God expels Adam and Eve from the garden and tells them: "By the sweat of your brow you will eat your food until you return to the ground, since from it you were taken; for dust you are and **to dust you will return.**" (Genesis 3:19)

Then the man on the island answers the serpent.

> "'You speak to me, but I cannot hear what thou say; I am before you, do you not know me?'
>
> Then the serpent took me in its mouth and carried me off to the place where it was wont to rest, and it set me down there, having done me no harm whatsoever.
>
> I was sound and whole, and it had not carried away any portion of my body.
>
> And it opened its mouth to me while I was lying flat on my stomach, and it said unto me, 'Who has brought you here? Who has brought you here, O miserable one?
>
> Who has brought you to this island of the sea, the two sides of which are in the waves?'
>
> Then I made answer to the serpent, my two hands being folded humbly before it, and I said unto it, 'I am one who was travelling to the mines on a mission of the king in a ship that was one hundred and fifty cubits long, and fifty cubits in breadth, and it was manned by a crew of one hundred and fifty men, who were chosen from among the best sailors of Egypt.
>
> They had looked upon the sky, they had looked upon the earth, and their hearts were more understanding than the hearts of lions. They were able to say beforehand when a tempest was coming, and to tell when a squall was about to rise before it broke.
>
> The heart of every man among them was wiser than that of his neighbor, and the arm of each was stronger than that of his neighbor; there was not one weak man among them.
>
> Nevertheless, it blew a gale of wind whilst we were still on the sea and before we could make the land. A gale rose, which continued to increase in violence, and with it there came upon us a wave eight cubits high. A plank of wood was driven

towards me by this wave, and I seized it; and as for the ship, those who were therein perished and not one of them escaped alive except myself. And now behold me by your side! It was a wave of the sea that brought me to this island.'

And the serpent said unto me, 'Have no fear, have no fear, O little one, and let not your face be sad, now that you have ar- rived at the place where I am. Verily, God has spared your life, and you have been brought to this island where there is food.

There is no kind of food that is not here, and it is filled with good things of every kind. Verily, you shall pass month after month on this island, until you have come to the end of four months, and then a ship shall come, and there shall be therein sailors who are acquaintances of yours, and you shalt go with them to your country, and thou shalt die in thy native town.'

And the serpent continued, 'What a joyful thing it is for the man who has experienced evil fortunes, and has passed safely through them, to declare them!

I will now describe unto you some of the things that have hap- pened unto me on this island. I used to live here with my breth- ren, and with my children who dwelt among them; now my children and my brethren together numbered seventy-five.'"

The 75 serpents probably refers to the 75 forms that the god Ra can take.

"'I do not make mention of a little maiden who had been brought to me by fate. And a star fell from heaven, and these [i.e. his children, and his brethren, and the maiden] came into the fire which fell with it.

I myself was not with those who were burnt in the fire, and I was not in their midst, but I almost died of grief for them. And I found a place wherein I buried them all together.

Now, if you are strong, and your heart flourishes, you shall fill both your arms with your children, and you shall kiss your wife, and you shall see your own house, which is the most beautiful thing of all, and you shall reach your country, and you shall live therein again together with your brethren, and dwell therein.'

Then I cast myself down flat upon my stomach, and I pressed the ground before the serpent with my forehead, saying, 'I will describe your power to the King, and I will make him to understand your greatness. I will cause to be brought unto you the unguent and spices called aba, and hekenu, and inteneb, and khasait, and the incense that is offered up in the temples, whereby every god is propitiated. I will relate unto him the things that have happened unto me, and declare the things that have been seen by me through your power, and praise and thanksgiving shall be made unto you in my city in the presence of all the nobles of the country.

*I will **slaughter bulls** for you, and will offer them up as **burnt-offerings**, and I will pluck feathered fowl in your honor.'"*

In the last two phrases above we can read again the elusive descriptions of rituals of offering, descriptions that are misleading so as not to disclose the real elements of the ancient Egyptian ritual. In contrast to the way the Egyptians did it, those phrases above show exactly what we read in Bible's account of how to make offerings to the God of Israel, i.e., slaughtering animals and burning their meat at the altar.

"'And I will cause to come to you boats laden with all the most costly products of the land of Egypt, even according to what is done for a god who is beloved by men and women in a land far away, whom they know not.'

*Then the serpent smiled at me, and the things which I had said to it were regarded by it in its heart as nonsense, for it said unto me, 'You have not a very great store of myrrh in Egypt, and all that you have is incense. Behold, I am the Prince of Punt, and the myrrh which is therein belongs to me. And as for the heken which you have said you will cause to be brought to me, is it not one of the chief products of this island? And behold, it shall come to pass that when you have once departed from this place, you shall **never more see** this island, for it shall **disappear** into the waves.'"*

Above we have seen the resemblance to the story in Genesis when Adam and Eve were expelled forever from the Garden of Eden, which was paradise like the island in this Egyptian tale. Recall also that, in the beginning of the Genesis creation story, all that existed was a primeval water under heaven; it may not be a coincidence that in the Tale of the Shipwrecked Traveler, the island will revert to water when it is unmade.

"And in due course, even as the serpent had predicted, a ship arrived, and I climbed up to the top of a high tree, and I recognized those who were in it. Then I went to announce the matter to the serpent, but I found that it had knowledge thereof already. And the serpent said unto me, 'A safe journey, a safe journey, O little one, to your house. You shall see your children again. I beseech you that my name may be held in fair repute in your city, for verily this is the thing which I desire of thee.'

Then I threw myself flat upon my stomach, and my two hands were folded humbly before the serpent. And the serpent gave me a ship-load of things, namely, myrrh, heken, inteneb, khasait, thsheps and shaas spices, eye-paint (antimony), skins of panthers, great balls of incense, tusks of elephants, greyhounds, apes, monkeys, and beautiful and costly products of all sorts and kinds. And when I had loaded these things into the ship, and had thrown myself flat upon my stomach in order to give thanks unto it for the same, it spoke unto me, saying, 'Verily you shalt travel to your country in two months, and you shall fill both your arms with your children, and you shall renew your youth in your coffin.'

Then I went down to the place on the sea-shore where the ship was, and I hailed the bowmen who were in the ship, and I spoke words of thanksgiving to the lord of this island, and those who were in the ship did the same. Then we set sail, and we journeyed on and returned to the country of the King, and we arrived there at the end of two months, according to all that the serpent had said.

And I entered into the presence of the King, and I took with me for him the offerings which I had brought out of the island. And the King praised me and thanked me in the presence of the nobles of all his country, and he appointed me to be one of his bodyguard, and I received my wages along with those who were his regular servants.

Cast you your glance then upon me, O Prince, now that I have set my feet on my native land once more, having seen and experienced what I have seen and experienced. Hear you unto me, for verily it is a good thing to hear unto men. And the Prince said unto me, 'Make not yourself out to be perfect, my friend! Does a man give water to a fowl at daybreak which he is going to kill during the day?'

Here ended The Story of the Shipwrecked Traveler, which has been written from the beginning to the end thereof according to the text that has been found written in an ancient book.

It has been written [i.e. copied] *by Ameni-Amen-āa, a scribe with skilful fingers. Life, strength, and health be to him!*

The Tale of King Khufu's Court

This entertaining tale tells of the glorious reign of King Khufu (Cheops), seven centuries before its composition.

In the story, the king grows bored and asks his sons to tell him about the marvels of the past. One by one, they rise up to narrate fantastic stories full of magic.

The first stories are simple ones that do not satisfy the king, but then one of his sons makes a change, bringing in a wise man who foretells that three children will be sent by a god yet born to a mortal woman, and that they will rule over every land and even overthrow Khufu's dynasty. This last tale closely resembles the stories of the miraculous conception and prophesied worldwide dominion of Jesus Christ.

Our purpose in analyzing this tale is to provide further evidence that the Abrahamic texts were sourced from ancient Egyptian literature, specifically from ancient Egyptian literary texts. As this tale is fairly long, I will quote only parts of it.

We will begin with an excerpt from the first story narrated by Khufu's sons, in which someone performs magic that transforms a wax crocodile into a real one.

> "Ubaaner then told the steward to fetch him his casket made of ebony and silver-gold, which contained materials and instruments used in working magic, and when it was brought him, he took out some wax, and fashioned a figure of a crocodile seven spans long. He then recited certain magical words over the crocodile, and said to it, 'When the young man comes to bathe in my lake you shall seize him.' Then giving the wax crocodile to the steward, Ubaaner said to him, 'When the young man goes down to the lake to bathe according to his daily habit, you shall throw the crocodile into the water after him.'
>
> Having taken the crocodile from his master the steward departed."

After some verses we read,

> *"When the steward had furnished the lodge, she went there, and the young peasant paid her a visit. After leaving the lodge he went and bathed in the lake, and the steward followed him and threw the wax crocodile into the water; it immediately turned into a large crocodile 7 cubits (about 11 feet) long and seized the young man and swallowed him up."*

Clearly this is meant to be a fanciful tale. Note the similarities between this tale and the tale of Moses and Aaron appearing before the king of Egypt:

> *"The Lord said to Moses and Aaron, 'When Pharaoh says to you, 'Perform a miracle,' then say to Aaron, 'Take your **staff and throw it down** before Pharaoh,' and **it will become a snake.'***
>
> *So, Moses and Aaron went to Pharaoh and did just as the Lord commanded. Aaron threw his staff down in front of Pharaoh and his officials, and it became a snake. Pharaoh then summoned wise men and sorcerers, and the Egyptian magicians also did the same things by their secret arts: Each one threw down his staff and it became a snake. But Aaron's staff swallowed up their staffs. Yet Pharaoh's heart became hard and he would not listen to them, just as the Lord had said."*

Another story told to king Khufu concerns a magician called Teta.

> *"'He is a certain peasant who is called Teta, and he lives in Tet-Seneferu. He is one hundred and ten years old, and up to this very day he eats five hundred bread-cakes, and a leg of beef, and drinks one hundred pots of beer.*
>
> *He knows how to reunite to its body a head which has been cut off, he knows how to make a lion follow him while the rope with which he is tied drags behind him on the ground, and he knows the numbers of the Apet chambers of the shrine of Thoth.'"*

Compare this to similar descriptions in the Bible of people living unrealistically long lives:

> *"After this, Job lived a **hundred and forty years**; he saw his children and their children to the fourth generation,"* (Job

*42:16) or "Altogether, Methuselah lived a total of **969 years**, and then he died." (Genesis 5:27)*

Later in the tale, after to have made many magical performances, the magician tells Khufu about the three children sent to earth by Ra.

"'The oldest of the three children of Rut-tetet shall bring it (a box with a secret about the god Thoth) to you.'

His Majesty said, 'It is my will that you shall tell me who this Rut-tetet is.'

Teta answered, 'This Rut-tetet is the wife of a priest of Rā of Sakhabu, who is about to give birth to three children of Rā.

He told her that these children should attain to the highest dignities in the whole country, and that the oldest of them should become high priest of Heliopolis.'

On hearing these words the heart of the king became sad."

First, as I said before, it is important to note that each city had its own god to worship; in this case, the residents of the city of Sakhbu worshiped the god Ra as their Lord.

Second, the meaning of the prediction that the eldest child will be "the high priest of Heliopolis" is that this child will be a king, replacing his dynasty, which explains why King Khufu became upset.

Later in the story, the magician opens a passage for the king through a water canal, in an episode that resembles the story of Moses opening the Red Sea waters for his followers.

"His Majesty asked, 'When will these three children be born?'

Teta answered, 'Rut-tetet will give them birth on the fifteenth day of the first month of Pert.'

The Majesty said, 'It's when the sandbanks of Two-Fish Canal are bare. My helper, if only I'd already passed it myself, to uphold the temple of Re Lord of Sakhbu!'

In reply Teta declared that he would take care that the water in the canal should be 4 cubits (about 6 feet) deep. (i.e. that the water should be deep enough for the royal barge to sail on the canal without difficulty.)

Later, the god Ra asks, on behalf of the King, other gods to help with the birth of the three children.

> *"When the day drew nigh in which the three sons were to be born, Rā, the Sun-god, ordered the four goddesses, Isis, Nephthys, Meskhenet, and Heqet, and the god Khnemu, to go and superintend the birth of the three children, so that when they grew up, and were exercising the functions of rule throughout all Egypt, they should build temples to them, and furnish the altars in them with offerings of meat and drink in abundance.*

> *Then the four goddesses changed themselves into the forms of dancing women, and went to the house wherein the lady Rut-tetet lay ill, and finding her husband, the priest of Rā, who was called Rāuser, outside, they clashed their cymbals together, and rattled their sistra, and tried to make him merry."*

The gods Isis, Nephthys, Meskhenet, Heqet, and Khnum are related to birthing. Then these gods were with Ruddjedet, who was giving birth.

> *"They went to the room wherein Rut-tetet lay. Isis, Nephthys, and Heqet assisted in bringing the three boys into the world. Meskhenet prophesied for each of them sovereignty over the land, and Khnemu bestowed health upon their bodies.*

> *After the birth of the three boys, the four goddesses and Khnemu went outside the house, and told Rāuser to rejoice because his wife Rut-tetet had given him three children."*

Then the gods produce "wonders" or miracles to prove that the gods have participated in the birth.

> *"'Then Isis said to her companions: "How is it that we who went to Rut-tetet [by the command of Rā] have worked no wonder for the children which we could have announced to their father, who allowed us to depart without begging a boon?'*

> *So, they made divine crowns such as belonged to the Lord (i.e. King), life, strength, health be to him! And they hid them in the barley. Then they sent rain and storm through the heavens, and they went back to the house of Rāuser..."*

This tale goes on after this, but we have enough now to compare it with the Christian stories of Jesus's conception and birth. Here, we can read the version of the tale from the Gospel of Matthew in the Bible.

"This is how the birth of Jesus the Messiah came about: His mother Mary was pledged to be married to Joseph, but before they came together, she was found to be pregnant through the Holy Spirit. Because Joseph her husband was faithful to the law, and yet did not want to expose her to public disgrace, he had in mind to divorce her quietly.

But after he had considered this, an angel of the Lord appeared to him in a dream and said, "Joseph son of David, do not be afraid to take Mary home as your wife, because what is conceived in her is from the Holy Spirit. She will give birth to a son, and you are to give him the name Jesus, because he will save his people from their sins."

*All this took place to fulfill what the Lord had said through the prophet: "The virgin will conceive and give birth to a son, and they will call him Immanuel" (which means **"God with us"**).*

When Joseph woke up, he did what the angel of the Lord had commanded him and took Mary home as his wife. But he did not consummate their marriage until she gave birth to a son. And he gave him the name Jesus.

*After Jesus was born in Bethlehem in Judea, during the time of King Herod, Magi from the east came to Jerusalem and asked, "Where is the one who has been **born king** of the Jews? We saw his star when it rose and have come to worship him."*

*When King **Herod heard this he was disturbed**, and all Jerusalem with him. When he had called together all the people's chief priests and teachers of the law, he asked them where the Messiah was to be born. "In Bethlehem in Judea," they replied, "for this is what the prophet has written:*

"'But you, Bethlehem, in the land of Judah, are by no means least among the rulers of Judah; for out of you will come a ruler who will shepherd my people Israel.'"

*Then Herod called the **Magi** secretly and found out from them the exact time the star had appeared. He sent them to*

Bethlehem and said, *"**Go and search carefully for the child.**
As soon as you find him, report to me, so that I too may go
and worship him."*

*After they had heard the king, they went on their way, and the
star they had seen when it rose went ahead of them until it
stopped over the place where the child was. When they saw
the star, they were overjoyed. On coming to the house, they
saw the child with his mother Mary, and they bowed down and
worshiped him.*

*Then they opened their treasures and presented him with gifts
of gold, frankincense, and myrrh. And having been warned in a
dream not to go back to Herod, they returned to their country
by another route."*

The Teaching of King Amenemhat I

For our final literary quotation, I chose a little excerpt of this Teaching because it depicts a deceased (and therefore divine) king speaking in a *revelation* to his son. Like every other ancient Egyptian Literary Text, this text was composed well after both kings (father and son) had died, and so both are addressed as gods.

> *"Beginning of the Teaching made by the Majesty of the Dual King Sehetepibra Son of Ra Amenemhat true of voice, declaring in a revelation of truth to his son the Lord of All, Saying,*
> *'Rise as God.*
> *Listen to what I tell you that you may be king of earth.*
> *That you may rule the river-banks.*
> *And achieve in excess of perfection."*

The meaning of the word "revelation" here is that the son is having a dream in which his father teaches him.

The concept of a divine revelation containing advice for how to live well on earth is reminiscent of the many Abrahamic texts featuring "revelations from God." Due to the understandable *confusion* due to the ancient Egyptians' multiple meanings for the word God, the Israelites probably mistook these ancient Egyptian works of fiction for true accounts of communication between gods and men, due to their unfortunate lack of familiarity with ancient Egyptian traditions.

Teaching of Amen-Em-Ope

This teaching is not in the same collection as the others, and I will not analyze it here because there are already many good analyses of it. It is worth mentioning, however, because other authors have concluded that this teaching is the source of much of the material in the Bible's Book of Proverbs as well as parts of other Old Testament texts including Deuteronomy and the Psalms.

In the early 20th century, when the connections between these works of literature were first discovered, mainstream scholars arrogantly assumed that Abrahamic monotheism was the source of the ancient Egyptian wisdom tradition.

W. O. E. Oesterley, a professor of Hebrew and Old Testament Exegesis at King's College London, was the author of *Wisdom of Egypt and the Old Testament in the Light of the Newly Discovered Teachings of Amen-em-ope*, which was first published by the London Society for Promoting Christian Knowledge in 1927. As we might expect from a Jewish, Christian, or Muslim author writing about the similarities between their ancestral culture and that of ancient Egypt, Oesterley attempted to undermine ancient Egyptian culture by presuming that the ancient Egyptians had copied from the Israelites in addition to the other way around: "Just as, on the one hand, specifically native Egyptian contributions to the world's cultural and religious progress penetrated into Palestine and were absorbed into the main stream of Hebrew religious development, so, on the other hand, certain results of the Semitic **genius** for religion in their turn penetrated into Egypt and contributed to the formulation of what was **highest and best** in Egyptian religion" (p. 106).

Oesterley's bias and prejudice are clear, but they cannot erase the fact that ancient Egyptian literature is older than Hebrew literature. If, as it appears, the Hebrew "prophets" actually borrowed the knowledge that they called divine from a foreign culture, their dishonesty makes their work not genius but rather fraud.

Pyramid Texts

Older than the others above is this last text, an excerpt of the pyramid text from the tomb of the last king of the Dynasty V, the Pharaoh Unas. He died in 2350 BCE and so the following text came to us from that time.

This text is different from the literary texts I used before because pyramid texts are one of those very sacred ones, where we can read many religious elements fully disclosed. One characteristic of the pyramid texts it is that they speculate the deceased individual living in the gods' realm, interacting with them.

It's important to note that pyramids texts were intended to be a guide and prayer for the deceased, and once they were placed inside the tomb only too few people had opportunity to read them. I'm stating it because through modern eyes people can think that they were intended to be used as political propaganda; perhaps the literary texts we studied before, which were popular and spread throughout ancient people, could have been used as political propaganda to spread awe on foreigners and potential enemies.

Remember that the ancient Egyptians believed that words have power to change reality, and this was why they prayed. In this following text you will read that they are presenting the deceased Pharaoh as the first god after the creator-God Atum; this was made to use that power of words to transform reality to make the deceased king great in the realm of the gods.

Another important thing to keep in mind is that the Egyptian sacred texts using of a symbolic language was not a kind of encryption; differently, they used their cosmology to create them, and only through their cosmology someone can understand the meaning of them.

Pay attention how the bible's accountings about Jesus in the after-life resembles, to say the less, this pyramid text.

> *"The sky has withdrawn the life of the star Septet (Sothis, the Dog-star); behold Unas a living being, the son of Septet. The Eighteen Gods have purified him in Meskha (the Great Bear), he is an imperishable star.*

The house of Unas perishes not in the sky, the throne of Unas perishes not on the earth. Men make supplication there; the gods fly here. Septet has made Unas fly to heaven to be with his brethren the gods. Nut (the sky-goddess), the Great Lady, has unfolded her arms to Unas. She has made them into two divine souls at the head of the Souls of Anu, under the head of Rā. She made them two weeping women when you were in your coffin.

The throne of Unas is by you, Rā, he yields it not up to anyone else. Unas comes forth into heaven by you, Rā. The face of Unas is like the faces of the Hawks. The wings of Unas are like those of geese. The nails of Unas are like the claws of the god Tuf. There is no evil word concerning Unas on earth among men. There is no hostile speech about him with the gods. Unas has destroyed his word, he has ascended to heaven. Upuatu has made Unas fly up to heaven among his brethren the gods. Unas has drawn together his arms like the Smen goose, he strikes his wings like a falcon, flying, flying. O men, Unas flies up into heaven.

O you gods of the West, O you gods of the East, O you gods of the South, O you gods of the North, you four groups who embrace the holy lands, devote you yourselves to Osiris when he appears in heaven. He shall sail into the Sky, with his son Horus by his fingers. He shall announce him, he shall make him rises up like the Great God in the Sky. They shall cry out concerning Unas: Behold Horus, the son of Osiris!

Behold Unas, the firstborn son of Hathor! Behold the seed of Geb! Osiris has commanded that Unas shall rise as a second Horus, and these Four Spirit-souls in Anu have written an edict to the two great gods in the Sky. Rā set up the Ladder in front of Osiris, Horus set up the Ladder in front of his father Osiris when he went to his spirit, one on this side and one on the other side; Unas is between them.

Behold, he is the god of the pure seats coming forth from the bath. Unas stands up, lo Horus; Unas sites down, lo Set. Rā grasps his hand, spirit to heaven, body to earth.

The skies lower, the Star-gods tremble, the Archers (groups of stars) quake, the bones of the Akeru (group of stars) gods tremble, and those who are with them are struck dumb when they see Unas rising up as a soul, in the form of the god who lives upon his fathers, and who turns his mother into his food. Unas is the lord of wisdom, and his mother knows not his name.

The adoration of Unas is in heaven, he has become mighty in the horizon like Temu, the father that gave him birth, and after Temu had given him birth Unas became stronger than his father. The Doubles (i.e. vital strength) of Unas are behind him, the soles of his feet are beneath his feet, his gods are over him, his serpents are seated upon his brow, the serpent-guides of Unas are in front of him, and the spirit of the flame looks upon his soul.

The powers of Unas protect him. Unas is a bull in heaven. He directs his steps where he wills. He lives upon the form which each god takes upon himself, and he eats the flesh of those who come to fill their bellies with the magical charms in the Lake of Fire. Unas is equipped with power against the spirit-souls thereof, and he rises in the form of the mighty one, the lord of those who dwell in power. Unas has taken his seat with his back turned towards Geb (the Earth-god). Unas has weighed his words (the judgement of the dead) with the hidden god who has no name, on the day of hacking in pieces the firstborn.

Unas is the lord of offerings, the untier of the knot, and he himself makes abundant the offerings of meat and drink. Unas devoures men, and lives upon the gods, he is the lord of envoys whom he sends forth on his missions. 'He who cuts off hairy scalps,' who dwells in the fields, ties the gods with ropes. Tcheser-tep shepherds them for Unas and drives them unto him; and the Cord-master has bound them for slaughter. Khensu, the slayer of the wicked, cuts their throats, and draws out their intestines, for it is he whom Unas sends to slaughter them, and Shesmu (the Osiris' executioner) cuts them in pieces, and boiled their members in his blazing caldrons of the night. Unas eats their magical powers, and he swallows their spirit-souls.

The great ones among them serve for his meal at daybreak, the lesser serve for his meal at eventide, and the least among them serve for his meal in the night. The old gods and the old

131

goddesses become fuel for his furnace. The mighty ones in heaven light the fire under the caldrons wherein are heaped up the thighs of the firstborn; and he who makes those who live in heaven to go about for Unas lights the fire under the caldrons with the thighs of their women; he goes about the Two Heavens in their entirety, and he goes round about the two banks of the Celestial Nile."

To understand those two stanzas above, where we read the king eating the gods flesh in the afterlife, we need to remember how they thought about the cosmos in a down-to-earth way. So, if here while living in flesh we need to feed ourselves from other living beings' substance in the afterlife what would be our sustenance? The divine god's matter. Even this speculation about the afterlife is in concordance to their theology's statement that the creator-God Atum divided himself (his own divine flesh) into millions and millions of beings and things. From these verses it is clear how they thought about the creation where we read *"The old gods and the old goddesses become fuel for his furnace."* It seems that in their religious philosophy, as well as each species of beings on earth can last forever but each individual need to bear, grow, and die, in the transcendental world it would happen in the same way. In few words, the earth's food chain is the manifestation and resemblance of that god Atum cut in his own divine flesh to create all beings.

Also, from the two verses above we can understand the purpose of their animal's sacrifice. Certainly, over the millennia their philosophy about it had been developed, but at that time we can see well-expressed in this text that they believed they could get the gods' power through the domination of their earthly manifestation, i.e., the animal's sacrifice.

One question more is, wouldn't be that the Jesus Christ Holy communion came from these ancient Egyptian religious beliefs as well? Read below the bible's excerpt from Mathew 26:

"While they were eating, Jesus took bread, and when he had given thanks, he broke it and gave it to his disciples, saying, 'Take and eat; this is my body.'

Then he took a cup, and when he had given thanks, he gave it to them, saying, 'Drink from it, all of you. This is my blood of the covenant, which is poured out for many for the forgiveness of sins. I tell you I will not drink from this fruit of the vine from now on until that day when I drink it new with you in my Father's kingdom.'"

Following, I continue the Pyramid Text we are reading here.

"Unas is the Great Power, the Power of Powers, and Unas is the Chief of the gods in visible forms. Whatsoever he finds upon his path he eats forthwith, and the magical might of Unas is before that of all the spirit-bodies who dwell in the horizon. Unas is the firstborn of the firstborn gods.

Unas is surrounded by thousands, and oblations are made unto him by hundreds; he is made manifest as the Great Power by Saah (Orion), the father of the gods. Unas repeats his rising in heaven, and he is crowned lord of the horizon. He has reckoned up the bandlets and the armrings of his captives, he has taken possession of the hearts of the gods. Unas has eaten the Red Crown, and he has swallowed the White Crown; the food of Unas is the intestines, and his meat is hearts and their words of power.

Behold, Unas eats of that which the Red Crown sends forth, he increases, and the words of power of the gods are in his belly; his attributes are not removed from him. Unas has eaten the whole of the knowledge of every god, and the period of his life is eternity, and the duration of his existence is everlastingness.

He is in the form of one who does what he wishes, and who does not do what he hates, and he abides on the horizon for ever and ever and ever. The Soul of the gods is in Unas, their spirit-souls are with Unas, and the offerings made unto him are more than those that are made unto the gods. The fire of Unas is in their bones, for their soul is in Unas, and their shades are with those who belong unto them. Unas has been with the two hidden Kha [...] gods, [...]; the seat of the heart of Unas is among those who live upon this earth for ever and ever and ever."

Solving the Mystery: Ancient Egyptian Fiction Poems Inspired the Sacred Abrahamic Texts

For more confirmation that my thesis is true, you can read the tales I quoted here in many sources as you find in the bibliography chapter. The more you read them, the more clearly you will see the truth of my argument. In those works, the authors helpfully provide dozens or even hundreds of notes for every poem, clarifying many passages that would otherwise be obscure to us because we are not familiar with ancient Egyptian narrative using customs, popular expressions, and euphemisms. The use of obscure words and expressions in the ancient Egyptian Literary Texts is not a coded expression of religious secrets, although many people today interpret the Abrahamic sacred texts in this way. Instead, it was a typical and popular means of communicating about the elements of everyday life. Even the symbolism of their sacred texts can be understood knowing ancient Egyptian cosmology, i.e., how they think the universe works.

Even reading only a few of those tales in addition to those I have quoted here, you will clearly see that the poems lack consistency, both individually and as a collection. This is because they were not composed to build a theology or promulgate a philosophy. Rather, they were composed for entertainment, for oral recitations, for spreading wisdom throughout society and for training scribes in how to read and write.

As we have seen in this book, ancient Egyptian philosophy, cosmogony, cosmology, and religion were written not in the Literary Texts but in the Sacred Texts, which were distinct from the Literary Texts in their careful symbolism, which stands in sharp contrast to the loose and hyperbolic language common in poems. More than that, the poems contain almost nothing related to actual religion, philosophy, cosmogony, and cosmology; not even real historic events are written factually. These poems are genuine fanciful works of fiction!

No ancient Egyptian would ever have taken these poems seriously as religious scriptures.

The evidence is overwhelming that the Israelites appropriated these poems under the mistaken impression that they were religious scriptures. But why did they do it?

In ancient times, Egypt was the most *envied* country. If any other people wanted to build a powerful nation or kingdom, they would surely have tried to copy the ancient Egyptians. In the Bible, likewise, we can read how the Israelites referred to ancient Egypt with awe, recognizing the superiority of Egyptian culture. We can even think that the ancient Egyptians used those fanciful texts to get reverence from foreigners.

As far as I have been able to determine through my extensive studies, the Israelites were not very well acquainted with real Egyptian religion, knowledge, or traditions. Thus, the Israelites took Egyptian literature seriously but interpreted it erroneously. This is why the Israelites confounded the characters of deceased kings who were considered gods with the actual creator-God. The Israelites imagined that, every time a deceased Egyptian king (ascribed as God) asked for allegiance and loyalty in a poem, it was actually a powerful God competing against other gods for human loyalty and winning. This mistake led the Israelites to shed blood for their God, slaughtering the devotees of all other gods, whereas the ancient Egyptians only went to war against foreigners for their Pharaoh, and never for any god.

Another misunderstanding is related to the method of offering sacrifices to God. The Abrahamic texts claim that God requires them to slaughter animals on altars and burn the animals' bodies in the fire, which is exactly what we read in ancient Egyptian Literary Texts written for entertainment. In contrast, the ancient Egyptians' Sacred Texts reveal that they never actually made their offerings like that.

Another more tragic misunderstanding is that the Israelites believed that wisdom teachings of human thinking had actually been sent by God; for this reason, the Israelites believed that every scrap of wisdom knowledge needed to be strictly enforced and that any deviation was punishable by death.

If the Israelites mistakenly appropriated the ancient Egyptian literary texts, I don't know if we can tell the same about the Christians who wrote the teachings and the life of Jesus Christ because not only many passages of Jesus Christ was written in the same fashion and used the same ancient Egyptian literary content as we read above but also the first Christians fled to live in Alexandria, in Egypt and in doing so they had access in some extent to ancient Egyptian sacred texts, even founding there the Christian Coptic Church, many centuries before the Catholic Church.

If you look at the Christian sacred rituals, you see that they come from the ancient Egyptian ones, the imagery, the use of fabrics to embellish the churches, priests and statuses, the habit to paint and scribe all of the interior of churches with phrases and paintings, the profound use of symbolic ritualistic ceremonies and the habit to use embalming to preserve the corpses of the dead popes and high priests inside the monumental churches. All of these came from ancient Egyptian tradition and religion and are prohibited by the Old Testament texts and it is the cause of the breakdown from the protestants with the Catholic Church centuries ago.

To conclude this section in a great style, I present you the 10 Abrahamic commandments in comparison to the 42 commandments of the ancient Egyptian goddess Ma'at. Remember that even the ancient Egyptians did not believe that these 42 commandments were directly *revealed* by the goddess. Everyone there understood that they had been developed by philosopher-priests.

The 10 Commandments X The 42 Commandments of Ma'at

"Provide for people, the herd of God. For their sake he made the sky and the earth; for them he drove away the darkness for the waters; he made the air of life so that they might breath. They are his likeness, who came from his flesh. For their sake he rises in the sky; for them he made the vegetation, small animals, birds and fish that feed them... When they weep, he hears... for God knows every name."

A wisdom text from *"The Instruction for King Merikare"* who ruled Egypt between 2075–2040 BC

Moses is said to have received these Ten Commandments from God when he was praying *alone* on a mountain. There is no consensus about the dates of Moses' life, but the accepted range is anywhere between 1592 BC and 1271 BC.

1. You shall have *no other Gods* but me.
2. You shall *not* make for yourself *any idol*, nor bow down to it or worship it.
3. You shall not misuse the name of the *Lord your God*.
4. You shall remember and keep the Sabbath day holy.
5. Respect your father and mother.
6. You must not commit murder.
7. You must not commit adultery.
8. You must not steal.
9. You must not give false evidence against your neighbor.
10. You must not be envious of your neighbor's goods. You shall not be envious of his house nor his wife, nor anything that belongs to your neighbor.

Ma'at had the following 42 commandments, recorded in the Papyrus of Ani as the 42 Negative Confessions.

1. I have not committed sin.
2. I have not committed robbery with violence.
3. I have not stolen.
4. I have not slain men and women.
5. I have not stolen grain.
6. I have not stolen offerings.
7. I have not stolen the property of the Gods.

8. I have not uttered lies.
9. I have not carried away food.
10. I have not uttered curses.
11. I have not committed adultery.
12. I have made none to weep.
13. I have not eaten the heart [i.e., I have not grieved uselessly, or felt remorse].
14. I have not attacked any man.
15. I am not a man of deceit.
16. I have not stolen cultivated land.
17. I have not been an eavesdropper.
18. I have slandered [no man].
19. I have not been angry without just cause.
20. I have not debauched the wife of any man.
21. I have not debauched the wife of [any] man. (repeats the previous affirmation but addressed to a different god).
22. I have not polluted myself.
23. I have terrorized none.
24. I have not transgressed [the Law].
25. I have not been wroth.
26. I have not shut my ears to the words of truth.
27. I have not blasphemed.
28. I am not a man of violence.
29. I am not a stirrer up of strife (or a disturber of the peace).
30. I have not acted (or judged) with undue haste.
31. I have not pried into matters.
32. I have not multiplied my words in speaking.
33. I have wronged none, I have done no evil.
34. I have not worked witchcraft against the King (or blasphemed against the King).
35. I have never stopped [the flow of] water.
36. I have never raised my voice (spoken arrogantly, or in anger).
37. I have not cursed (or blasphemed) God.
38. I have not acted with evil rage.
39. I have not stolen the bread of the gods.
40. I have not carried away the khenfu cakes from the spirits of the dead.
41. I have not snatched away the bread of the child, nor treated with contempt the god of my city.
42. I have not slain the cattle belonging to the god.

You can see that the moral commandments of Moses come from the 42 Commandments of Ma'at he knew from ancient Egyptian tradition wherein he grew up. It cannot be said that the moral commandments between those ten came to Moses' knowledge from God.

Conclusion

If we want to describe the Abrahamic sacred texts and the religions that have developed from these texts in a few words, we can call them inconsistent and unreliable. The texts themselves are so inconsistent that no follower of any of the three Abrahamic religions, Judaism, Christianity, and Islam, can put in practice everything that their scriptures prescribe.

Because these scriptures were largely drawn from Egyptian literary poems, which were meant to entertain and which accordingly contained the exaggeration and hyperbole that are typical of poetry, the confusion within and between texts requires Abrahamic priests and devotees to work hard to interpret them to piece together a coherent theology, cosmogony, cosmology, and system of worship. This is extremely difficult given that the ancient Egyptian literary texts, and the Abrahamic religious scriptures that they inspired, contain nothing that can serve as a reliable theology on which to build a religion.

The consequence of this is that there is so much contradictory information in the Abrahamic scriptures that everyone can find whatever they are looking for. Thus, every follower has a different interpretation of what is right, yet all have the conviction that their version of what is right is worth killing or dying for. One esteems only the wisdom literature; another takes the poems as literal descriptions of the universe (these are the "fundamentalists"). But if you pay attention, you will see that even the fundamentalist cannot practice exactly what is written in the texts, because, again, they are incoherent! This is why there have been so many schisms within each Abrahamic religion, so that, today, there are many branches fighting with each other.

As the rituals prescribed in the Abrahamic texts are deemed unacceptable, the high priests of each religion have had to invent rituals for themselves. The most interesting of these is that of the Catholic Church, whose rituals and customs are fairly similar to those of ancient Egyptian religion, although the Bible prohibits them from embracing other religions. Like the ancient Egyptian rituals,

Catholic ceremonies are highly symbolic, using many emblematic sacred tools, costumes and objects, and relying heavily on the power of words and performative actions. Even the Catholic Church temples are a reproduction of the ancient Egyptian ones, fully carved and painted in colorful pictures and inscriptions!

With regard to statues we can read about their prohibition in Exodus 20:

> *"You shall not make for yourself an image in the form of anything in heaven above or on the earth beneath or in the waters below. You shall not bow down to them or worship them; for I, the Lord your God, am a jealous God, punishing the children for the sin of the parents to the third and fourth generation of those who hate me, but showing love to a thousand generations of those who love me and keep my commandments."*

But just as the tools used in worship were important to the ancient Egyptians, the Catholic Church has never given up using them! The Catholic Church has even employed the power of sacred statues and mummified corpses to maintain an open link between the earth and the realm of the gods: have not only all of the popes been embalmed and buried inside monumental churches, but Catholics have a long tradition of making pilgrimages, sacred journeys, to the burial sites of their saints to be healed or blessed. Perhaps this *accidental* adherence to ancient Egyptian ways is why the Catholic Church has survived for so many years as the ancient Egyptian civilization did.

How did the Catholic Church acquire the ancient Egyptian rituals? Remember that Mark the Evangelist was said to have lived in Egypt and that the first Christian church was the Coptic Church in Alexandria, which persists even today. Thus, the medieval and modern Catholic ceremonies came from ancient Egyptian culture.

The Source of This Confusion. As we have seen in our literary investigation, the Israelites were unfortunately not acquainted with genuine Egyptian religion, knowledge, and traditions. Thus, the Israelites took Egyptian entertainment literature seriously as religious scriptures. This mistake has led the Israelites to shed blood for their *God*, attempting to eliminate the devotees of all other gods. Ancient Egyptians, in contrast, only went to war against foreigners for their Pharaoh to protect their country, and never for any god. The ancient Egyptians never fought over religion!

There is no Abrahamic God. In our theological investigation we have seen that the Abrahamic texts admit the existence of many gods, beginning with the story of the Garden of Eden. It is a lie to say that the Abrahamic texts tell us that only one god exists in the universe.

In our theological probe we determined that no human is wise enough to confirm that he or she has seen a god or a god's envoy as opposed to some other kind of spirit. Whenever someone claims that he or she has seen a god or a god's envoy, it always remains possible that the apparition was in fact a demon, a being weaker than the gods yet powerful enough to shock humans with flashy visions and vulgar "miracles." As we have discussed, the gods' actions, powerful as they are, are visible in the form of the creation around us, including the stars, the planets, the galaxies, the many living beings, every physical law, force, or substance and even social laws and powers such as the Social Power we have analyzed above. Every genuine god's creations and manifestations are visible and available to everyone, and everyone is under their rule, just as we are all subject to the laws of physics. Therefore, every time someone claims to have witnessed a miracle that was performed outside the general laws of physics in the presence of that person alone, this "miracle" was certainly performed by a demon. Sadly, many people believe that these showy but ephemeral and pathetic demon apparitions are even more reliably divine than the genuine work of the gods.

Unfortunately, for the last two millennia, all humanity has suffered the consequences of belief in the arrogant and imprudent claims that God has commanded individuals to impose loyalty to God on other people through any means, including genocide.

Abrahamic Religions are Barbaric in its Essence. Many people rise some arguments against this book's thesis telling that we can encounter many good deeds inside the Abrahamic civilizations.

I agree that we find many great endeavors produced within Abrahamic societies. But most of them are not an Abrahamic outcome, in contrast, most of those great works came from Roman, Greek and ancient Egyptian tradition, as we can see inside the Christendom for centuries; the majority of them were fashioned regardless of the Abrahamic tradition. The legislation came from Roman institutions, the culture, and arts derived from Greek-Roman tradition, the religious rituals from ancient Egyptians, all of them polytheistic civilizations. Or the great achievements come as a result of the Scientific Revolution, i.e., from something outside and regardless of religion. They are so in opposition to Abrahamic texts that the Jews and the Muslims scorn them, even remember that the protestants broke with the Catholic Church for this reason.

They are so in opposition to Abrahamic texts that the Jews and the Muslims scorn them, even remember that the protestants broke with the Catholic Church for this reason.

Islamic priests and scholars all the time state that they are "more Christians" than the Christians themselves when they read the Abrahamic texts and see Christians following traditions forbidden by the Bible's prophets.

If something can be assured about Islam is that it is really wiping out all the other ancient traditions from its civilization and put in practice only the Abrahamic custom in every aspect of their lives.

One of the most truthful explanations of what civilization is it's to say that civilization is the attempt to reduce the violence into being the last resort to solve human problems. What we see inside the Abrahamic civilization is that, without the polytheistic Roman, Greek or Egyptian cultural developments and achievements, its outcome is always oppression, torture and genocides.

It is true that there were violence inside the ancient traditions, but the civilization is not the end of violence, it is the **attempt** to reduce it to a minimum we can, but inside the Abrahamic texts as everyone can read there is nothing bounded to put violence as a last resort while, in contrast, it can be seen in ancient traditions like Roman, Greek and the Egyptian. In their essence the Abrahamic tradition is barbaric, i.e., it has violence in its heart and as its principles.

The "*Great*" Demon's Creation. If it is even true that a spirit of some kind appeared to the Abrahamic "prophets," therefore, it must have been a demon. This demon has inspired the conflagration of our modern world by sowing the seeds of monotheistic intolerance and hatred to such an extent that our culture ended up separating religion from everything else, beginning with science, then moving on to state affairs, and finally all of human life, which is how materialism was born.

Whereas many people believed that materialism was their salvation from oppressive religion, the Abrahamic demon saw that materialism was actually the apex of his achievement and a necessary step toward his goal of spreading genocide throughout the world, as materialism affirms that the universe is a dumb and senseless creation and that human intelligence is the only good thing to emerge from it. Thus, it is entirely up to humans to rectify this atrocious universe. Yet all materialistic doctrines share the same Abrahamic principles, such as requiring loyalty to an intellectual idea which is the only way to save humanity from this miserably savage world, or, in Abrahamic words, from hell. The result was, as an example, World War II and the period after the war during which many governments slaughtered their own people in the name of a materialistic doctrine, accounting for the brutal deaths of more than 100 million people in just a few years.

The regrettable conclusion is that all of humanity is now living under the biggest fraud in human history, a fraud that is responsible for the greatest crimes against humanity in our history: oppression, torture, slaughter, and genocide in the name of a false god, who cannot be anything but a demon, who is thirsty for human suffering and blood, who would do anything to turn us away from the true gods, to cloud our natural desire to live in order and harmony, and to force us to live the most profane life possible.

This great and long-lasting crime against humanity could not have originated in any being but a demon. Yet this demon envies the gods, because he has no power of his own. His power only comes from deceiving people and forcing them to act on his behalf. Once he is exposed in his raw evil, envy, greed, and weakness, no good-hearted person will follow him anymore.

Acknowledgments

First of all, I express my thanks to the great and glorious god Djehuty, the god of divine words, knowledge, wisdom, for being with me during this work and during all my life; you have never left me alone.

"May Djehuty receive this book as an offering for his joy.

Praise to Djehuty, the son of Ra, the Moon beautiful in his rising, Lord of Bright Appearing who illuminates the gods.

Hail to you, Djehuty, who spreads out the seat of the gods, who knows their mysteries and establishes their commands; He who sifts evidence, who makes the evil deed rise up against the doer, who judges all humankind.

Praise to Djehuty, from whom evil flees, who accepts him, who avoids evil, the Vizier who gives judgment, who vanquishes crime and recalls all that is forgotten, the one who remembers both time and eternity.

Praise to Djehuty whose words endure forever!"

I thank each one of the dedicated Egyptologists who have brought the gifted civilization of ancient Egypt to light again after so many centuries of oblivion.

May you drink the beer of gods,

may you eat the food given to you by the gods,

may you rest in the place and the shadow in the company of the gods!

I thank every scholar whose works were useful in guiding me along the right path to reach the goal of accessing this knowledge and writing this book.

May you drink the beer of gods,

may you eat the food given to you by the gods,

may you rest in the place and the shadow in the company of the gods!

147

I thank each editor who worked over this book to make it better for readers. Special greetings to Cathy Suter, Enago's professionals, Mary from Miblart, and Benjamin from Damonza.

May you drink the beer of gods,

may you eat the food given to you by the gods,

may you rest in the place and the shadow in the company of the gods!

I thank the millions of ancient Egyptians, the justified, whose philosophy, cosmogony, cosmology, and religion, whose truly divine discoveries and developments, made it possible for them to craft their long-lasting, great, and prosperous civilization and who still gift us with their divine, reliable, and consistent knowledge which no one can deny; even those who dislike them still copy their wisdom.

May you drink the beer of gods,

may you eat the food given to you by the gods,

may you rest in the place and the shadow in the company of the gods!

I thank every person whose passage through my life has helped me to walk the right path to reach the goal of acquiring this knowledge and writing this book.

May you drink the beer of gods,

may you eat the food given to you by the gods,

may you rest in the place and the shadow in the company of the gods!

I thank you, the readers who have accepted the invitation to accompany me on this deep journey by reading my book and who have, by doing so, been awakened forever.

May you drink the beer of gods,

may you eat the food given to you by the gods,

may you rest in the place and the shadow in the company of the gods!

Life, Prosperity, and Health!

You are endowed, o reader, with the power of the word

I invite every reader to use any part of the text below to assist me in spreading the knowledge of the ancient Egyptian philosophers across the world: May Ma'at manifests herself throughout the world.

You have the power of words in your hands to change the way we are living, to orient our lives toward truth, harmony, order, justice, beauty, equilibrium, and peace. Spread the message of the ancient Egyptian tradition and religion in every way you can, through flyers, social media posts, meetings, etc. You have the power in your tongue.

We need your help. The ancient Egyptians who sought to bring peace and harmony to the world were silenced many centuries ago by Judaism, Christianity, and Islam through oppression and the sword.

Never in all of human history has more human blood been shed than under the rule of Abrahamic religions. Our modern times have been recognized as a time of everlasting intolerance, hatred, and genocide.

Most people do not understand that it does not need to be like this. They do not know the ancient Egyptian philosophy that had been vanished from Earth. Now that Egyptologists have rediscovered it, we have access to another way to solve human problems. The key is to use the ancient Egyptian reliable way of thinking.

The lords of war silenced ancient Egyptian tradition and civiliza-tion because no one would have supported their warmongering if they had known about any alternative. The belligerent brutally destroyed a civilization that had endured for more than 5,000 years to replace it with a civilization whose norm, whose main command-ment, is to sacrifice other humans.

Take this book, read it, and, if we deserve your help, assist us in spreading this knowledge to awaken people, to shift the way we are living away from intolerance, hatred, and human sacrifice and toward harmony, justice, order, beauty, equilibrium and peace.

Thank you very much,

Eloy Rodrigo Colombo

May Ma'at manifests herself in your life!

Please, dear reader, let your review in the platform where you acquired the book. Now you know that every word counts!

Bibliography

The Holy Bible, New International Version® NIV®. Biblica, Inc.

Conrad, Chris. *Why did Jesus Have to Die? It's not what you think.* Lulu, 2016

Roberts, J. Stephen. *Why does the Heathen Rage? A Novel of the Crusades.* Self-published, 2016

Lewisohn, Ludwig. *The Island Within.* Syracuse University Press, 1997

Twain, Mark. *Joan of Arc.* Ignatius Press, 2007

Kurt Lewin. *Resolving Social Conflicts and Field Theory in Social Science.* American Psychological Association, 2000

Smith, Wolfgang. *The Quantum Enigma.* Angelico Press / Sophia Perenis, 2011

Twain, Mark. *The Innocents Abroad.* The Seawolf Press, 2018

Deely, John. *Four Ages of Understanding: The First Postmodern Survey of Philosophy from Ancient Times to the Turn of the Twenty-First Century.* University of Toronto Press, 2001

Kirsch, Jonathan. *The God Against Gods: The History of the War Between Monotheism and Polytheism.* Penguin Books, 2004.

Assmann, Jan. *The Search for God in Ancient Egypt.* Lorton, David transl. Cornell University Press, 2001, 1984.

Allen, James P. *Middle Egyptian: An Introduction to the Language and Culture of Hieroglyphs.* Cambridge University Press, 2000.

Wilkinson, Richard H. *The Complete Gods and Goddesses of Ancient Egypt.* Thames & Hudson, 2003.

Silverman, David P. *Divinity and Deities in Ancient Egypt.* Cornell University Press, 1991

David, Rosalie. *Religion and Magic in Ancient Egypt.* Penguin, 2002.

Teeter, Emily. *Cults: Divine Cults.* Cambridge University Press, 2001.

Dunand, Françoise; Zivie-Coche, Christiane. *Gods and Men in Egypt: 3000 BCE to 395 CE.* Lorton, David transl. Cornell University Press, 2005.

Shafer, Byron E, ed. *Temples of Ancient Egypt.* IB Tauris, 1997.

Montserrat, Dominic. *Akhenaten: History, Fantasy and Ancient Egypt.* Routledge, 2000.

Najovits, Simson. *Egypt, trunk of the tree.* Algora Publishing, 2003

Reidy, Richard J. *Eternal Egypt: Ancient Rituals for the Modern World.* iUniverse, 2010

Reidy, Richard J. *Everlasting Egypt: Kemetic Rituals for the Gods.* iUniverse 2018

Pinch, Geraldine. *Magic in Ancient Egypt.* University of Texas Press, 2010

Ritner, Robert Kriech. *The Mechanics of Ancient Egyptian Magical Practice.* The University of Chicago, 2008.

Wallis Budge, E. A. *The Literature of the Ancient Egyptians.* London J.M. Dent & Sons Limited Aldine House, 1914. You can download free the pdf in this link: www.gutenberg.org/ebooks/15932

The Loyalist Teaching transliteration and translation: www.ucl.ac.uk/museums-static/digitalegypt/literature/loyalist/text.html

The Teaching of King Amenenhat I, transliteration and translation: https://www.ucl.ac.uk/museums-static/digitalegypt//literature/teachinga1sec1.html

R.B., Parkinson. *The Tale of Sinuhe and Other Ancient Egyptian Poems: 1940 – 1640 BC.* Oxford University Press, 1997.

Oesterley, W. O. E. *Wisdom of Egypt and the Old Testament in the Light of the Newly Discovered Teachings of Amen-em-ope.* Kessinger Publishing, LLC, 2010.

Pinch, Geraldine. *Egyptian Mythology: A Guide to the Gods, Goddesses, and Traditions of Ancient Egypt.* Oxford University Press, 2002.

Manley, Bill. *Egyptian Hieroglyphs for Complete Beginners.* Thames & Hudson, 2012.

Silverman, David P., et al. *Ancient Egypt.* Oxford University Press, 1997.

Wilkinson, Richard H. *The Complete Temples of Ancient Egypt.* Thames & Hudson, 2000.

Dr. Ogden Goelet, Jr, et al. *The Egyptian Book of the Dead: The Book of Going Forth by Day.* Chronicles Books, 2015.

Roberts, Allen E. *The Craft and its Symbols: Opening the Door to Masonic Symbolism.* Macoy Publishing and Masonic Supply Company, Inc., 1974.

Koltro-Rivera, Mark E. *Freemasonry: An Introduction.* Penguin Group, 2011.

Earnshaw, Christopher. *Freemasonry: Spiritual Alchemy.* Author's Proof, 2019.

De Biasi, Jean-Louis. *Esoteric Freemasonry: Rituals & Practices for a Deeper Understanding.* Llewellyn Publications, 2018.

Lewis, Harvey Spencer. *Master of the Rose Cross: A Collection of Essays by and about Harvey Spencer Lewis.* Supreme Grand Lodge of The Ancient and Mystical Order Rosae Crucis, 2015.

Edwards, Lonnie C. *Spiritual Laws that Govern Humanity and the Universe.* Supreme Grand Lodge of The Ancient and Mystical Order Rosae Crucis, 2015.

Rebisse, Christian et al. *Rosicrucian Digest, Volume 92, number 1: Martinism.* Supreme Grand Lodge of The Ancient and Mystical Order Rosae Crucis, 2014

Maggid, Joshua et al. *Rosicrucian Digest, Volume 90, number 2: Kabbalah.* Supreme Grand Lodge of The Ancient and Mystical Order Rosae Crucis, 2012.

Tolle, Eckhart. *The Power of Now: A Guide to Spiritual Enlightenment.* Namaste Publishing and New World Library, 1997.

Guénon, René. *The Reign of Quantity & the Signs of the Times.* Sophia Perennis, 2004.

Juvenel, Bertrand. *On Power: The Natural History of its Growth.* Liberty Fund, 1976.

Guénon, René. *Symbols of Sacred Science.* Sophia Perennis, 2004.

Ortega y Gasset, José. *The Revolt of the Masses.* Oxford University Press, 1932.

Synopsis

The genuine and intrepid Colombo continues bringing us the knowledge possessed only by an elite over the Earth.

In his new original and astonishing book, he journeys back to ancient times to show us how humanity has derailed from ancient to modern times such that our world is now characterized by:

- Intolerance
- Hatred
- Genocide

How did we get into this state? Since in ancient times the major conflicts in life were political ones, restricted to the elite in society, and military conflicts, restricted to the armies; the common people were typically spared. Thus, even a complete government turnover typically left a civilization' gods, culture and habits intact; in other words, they were sacred and untouchable.

Within those polytheistic societies, people could live diverse traditions and worship different gods freely and in peace.

One of those great civilizations was ancient Egypt that lasted for more than 3000 years!

The question is what actually destroyed the formidable ancient Egyptian civilization, which was more tolerant and harmonious than our own?

The author went beyond a simple answer to that question revealing *who* was responsible for annihilating both ancient Egypt and the Roman civilization: two prosperous civilizations that had thrived for millennia. The culprit is Abrahamic monotheism, and especially Christianity.

Different from today, in ancient times, everything was regarded as falling under the purview of religion. This meant that religion was not seen as an optional add-on to life; rather, religion was life. Only an alternate religion that demanded absolute loyalty to the point of death, such as an Abrahamic religion, could have destroyed such a compelling civilization that had lasted for millennia.

Under the monotheistic Abrahamic religions, however, this was not the case, as everyone can read in the first commandment issued by the "God of Israel":

> *"You shall have **no other Gods** but me." (Exodus 20)*

Furthermore, this god issued clear instructions for when anyone disagreed with his teachings:

> *"If your brother, the son of your mother, or your son or your daughter or the wife you embrace or your friend who is as your own soul entices you secretly, saying, 'Let us go and **serve other gods**,' which neither you nor your fathers have known, some of the **gods of the peoples** who are around you, whether near you or far off from you, from the one end of the earth to the other, you shall not yield to him or listen to him, nor shall your eye pity him, nor shall you spare him, nor shall you conceal him. But **you shall kill him**." (Deuteronomy 13)*

Under this system, anyone who embraced the Abrahamic faith was required to fulfill all of the God of Israel's orders without questioning.

Once even the Roman emperors had converted to Christianity, not only were the thriving polytheistic civilizations of Rome and Egypt doomed, but all of Western civilization was bound to obey these terrible commands.

The rise of Christianity was not a mere political power transfer but the extermination of entire civilizations. Since then, the three Abrahamic religions have required more human sacrifice than any other system in history. Why do people overlook this?

As the fate of the world has been largely determined by the Abrahamic religions, we need to investigate them in depth. The author has found that the Abrahamic sacred texts actually derive from ancient Egyptian wisdom literature. In this book, the author fearlessly leads you on a journey into the world of ancient Egyptian philosophy, which is the only reliable way to understand the Abrahamic sacred texts as they were meant to be read.

This examination leads to a shocking question. Are the Abrahamic sacred texts, including the Jewish Torah, the Christian Bible, and the Islamic Quran, a case of accidental plagiarism or intentional fraud?

As the Abrahamic sacred texts are not genuine, we must ask who, if anyone, really appeared to the prophets. And who is responsible for the miracles reported in the Abrahamic scriptures?

The answers are chilling and unforgettable.

The Author

Eloy Rodrigo Colombo is a scholar whose studies in philosophy, theology, economics, and history have led him to the conclusions presented in his astonishing and unforgettable works.

This is his second book; his first is "No One Can Escape the 4 Laws," a work wherein he shows how the four main laws of economics, discovered by the French economic genius León Walras in 1860, have the power to explain every economic phenomenon present in our lives.

Colombo is an indefatigable truth-seeker. In this book, he has dared to reveal the roots of the modern problems of intolerance, hatred, and genocide. Although these problems seem insurmountable, he reveals the shocking truth: monotheism as practiced by the three Abrahamic religions, namely, Judaism, Christianity, and Islam, is the source of all these modern problems.

As long as the Abrahamic way of thinking reigns supreme, humanity will remain immersed in intellectual corruption such that every people will continue to say they want peace while actually working to wipe their rivals off the face of the earth.

He in His Own Words

"My Path Toward this Book"

Who didn't at least once in your life think about the origins of the universe, cosmos, and life, when lying outside and gazing toward the infinite sky? And, who has not once questioned whether there is some superior being behind all the creation?

Some people give up the effort to find the answers assuming a cynical approach to live with; a lame and blind way to live, to say the least, as transcendence is part of life, rather it is immanent in reality; to realize that someone just needs to quietly stare at the infinite sky, and those questions will naturally arise again.

I have even tried to liv a cynical life, but I couldn't keep at it; I couldn't give up finding some clue, at least some coherence, in all of what we call reality.

Does every way lead you to Rome? No, to ancient Egypt!

The more I was studying philosophy, religion, and history, the more I was being sent to ancient Egypt.

For example, do you know whence the symbol of medicine, i.e., two snakes winding around an often winged staff come ? The answer is from ancient Egyptian philosophical developments. The snake is one of the depictions of Sekhmet, the goddess of plagues for whom they prayed asking her to appease the diseases.

So, if you make an effort to follow the clues, everything will send you to ancient Egypt.

But don't think that it was easy for me. No, you know we are modern people who are educated to generally scorn toward ancient people. We believe that we are at the apex of humankind. It would be required of me to jump through the abyss of modern obscurantism to reach the other neglected side.

In fact, our modern apex is our arrogance in enriching our cynical lives with some ancient people's meanings without crediting them for it.

Something was wrong in modern works.

I could not help to suspect that something was wrong when I read many books, from freemasonry to mystic schools such as Rosicrucian, Martinism, and Kabbalah.

A fundamental question arose: how could those mystic schools mix Abrahamic monotheism with ancient Egyptian polytheism as Abrahamic texts teach that *"You shall have **no other Gods** but me,"* as we read in Exodus 20?

I realized that those mystic schools with no exception were blending the utterly immiscible Abrahamic religions with the ancient Egyptian one.

Religious people answer this interrogation telling you that the Abrahamic teachings were composed using symbols and that we are required to decipher them.

"To decipher?" I thought. How to decipher the clear commandments and teachings like this one below?

> *"If your brother, the son of your mother, or your son or your daughter or the wife you embrace or your friend who is as your own soul entices you secretly, saying, 'Let us go and serve other gods,' which neither you nor your fathers have known, some of the gods of the peoples who are around you, whether near you or far off from you, from the one end of the earth to the other, you shall not yield to him or listen to him, nor shall your eye pity him, nor shall you spare him, nor shall you conceal him. But **you shall kill him**."*

The Bible is full of similar verses like in Deuteronomy 13 above. The prophets stated nothing to be decoded in such a strict lesson! Anyone who sincerely reads them knows it.

But the schools cited before, insist that they are interpreting the Abrahamic sacred symbols in the texts. And one of the most famous works in interpreting the Abrahamic symbols is the book "The Zohar," which is the source of Kabbalah. The problem is that this book also needs for its turn to be deciphered as it was written using symbols as well.

I started getting anxious to answer the question, "What are they trying to cover with all of those excuses regarding the truth of the Abrahamic text and all those perpetual interpretations?" and "Why are they doing it?"

I could not avoid inquiring the critical matter "What if the being they behold as a good God was, in reality, an evil being, maybe a demon?" Because this being requires his followers to make human sacrifices throughout the Bible's texts and even this God on his own named himself "God of hosts" many times in those texts.

Furthermore, while the Abrahamic God requires his followers to commit horrible crimes, he calls the other gods demons.

Why do the followers of the Abrahamic faiths call them demons, if the ancient Egyptian gods never requested any kind of crime from his followers, not to cite other religions?

What was and is happening? A kind of hypnosis? Because how is it possible that an evil being is identifying himself as God, the only good being in the universe, if he asks people to kill any other gods' followers, and people obey him without question and even believe they are doing a good thing.

Something was terribly wrong. The more I studied the Abrahamic texts, the redder from human blood was this God's clothes.

Although this was a tough turning point in my findings, finally, I had been able to jump through the modern abyss of lies to reach the other side beyond this obscurantism.

And the more I studied the ancient Egyptian philosophy, theology, religions, and other texts, the more amazed I became. How down-to-earth they were. How responsible they had been toward life and their own deeds.

I came to realize the reason why they were capable of building a civilization that endured for more than 3000 years. Think of it; today, we are struggling to have a stable 4-year government.

If I could summarize in some words the ancient Egyptian goals, I could tell:

- Truth
- Justice
- Order
- Harmony
- Beauty
- Cosmic Equilibrium

They were meticulous about the words, and they had already understood that perfection is not for us, humans; instead, they realized that we are just capable of developing the meaning of cosmic equilibrium and trying to achieve that. However, perfection is out of our scope and reality.

The ancient Egyptians were so developed that until today we borrow their symbols to enrich our lives with some meaning. But, sadly, what we have from them are only void depictions.

It's time for you to know their marvelous intellectual achievements, as I did.

I invite you to go ahead, and I promise that I will not disappoint you with the journey into the ancient Egyptian times I'm glad to have created to share with you all.

Life, Prosperity, and Health.

Made in the USA
Coppell, TX
13 August 2023

20309771R00111